Creation
and
Evolution

Creation and Evolution

Universal Forces Shaping Humankind

By Edgar Cayce

A.R.E. Press • Virginia Beach • Virginia

A.R.E. Press
215 67th Street
Virginia Beach, VA 23451-2061

ISBN-13: 978-0-87604-956-3

Cover design by Richard Boyle

Contents

Foreword
Who Was Edgar Cayce?

Edgar Cayce (1877-1945) has been called "the Sleeping Prophet," "the father of Holistic medicine," "the miracle man of Virginia Beach," and "the most documented psychic of all time." For forty-three years of his adult life, he had the ability to put himself into some kind of self-induced sleep state by lying down on a couch, closing his eyes, and folding his hands over his stomach. This state of relaxation and meditation enabled him to place his mind in contact with all time and space and gave him the ability to respond to any question he was asked. His responses came to be called "readings" and contain insights so valuable that even to this day Edgar Cayce's work is known throughout the world. Hundreds of books have explored his amazing psychic gift, and the entire range of Cayce material is accessed by tens of thousands of people daily via the Internet.

Although the vast majority of the Cayce material deals with health and every manner of illness, countless topics were explored by Cayce's psychic talent: dreams, philosophy, intuition, business advice, the Bible, education, childrearing, ancient civilizations, personal spirituality, improving human relationships, and much more. In fact, during Cayce's lifetime he discussed an amazing 10,000 different subjects, and the

Edgar Cayce database of readings (available to A.R.E. members via the web) consists of a mind-boggling 24 million words!

The Cayce legacy presents a body of information so valuable that Edgar Cayce himself might have hesitated to predict its impact on contemporary society. Who could have known that eventually terms such as meditation, auras, spiritual growth, reincarnation, and holism would become household words to millions? Edgar Cayce's A.R.E. (the Association for Research and Enlightenment, Inc.) has grown from its humble beginnings to an association with Edgar Cayce Centers in countries around the world. Today, the Cayce organizations consist of hundreds of educational activities and outreach programs, children's camps, a publishing company, membership benefits and services, volunteer contacts and programs worldwide, massage and health services, prison and prayer outreach programs, conferences and workshops, Internet and online activities, and affiliated schools (Atlantic University: AtlanticUniv.edu and the Cayce/Reilly School of Massage: CayceReilly.edu).

Edgar Cayce was born and reared on a farm near Hopkinsville, Kentucky. He had a normal childhood in many respects. However, he could see the glowing energy patterns that surround individuals. At a very early age he also told his parents that he could see and talk with his grandfather—who was deceased. Later, he developed the ability to sleep on his schoolbooks and retain a photographic memory of their entire contents.

As the years passed, he met and fell in love with Gertrude Evans, who would become his wife. Shortly thereafter, he developed a paralysis of the vocal cords and could scarcely speak above a whisper. Everything was tried, but no physician was able to locate a cause. The laryngitis persisted for months. As a last resort hypnosis was tried. Cayce put myself to sleep and was asked by a specialist to describe the problem. While asleep he spoke normally, diagnosing the ailment and prescribing a simple treatment. After the recommendations were followed, Edgar Cayce could speak normally for the first time in almost a year! The date was March 31, 1901—that was the first reading.

When it was discovered what had happened, many others began to want help. It was soon learned that Edgar Cayce could put himself into this unconscious state and give readings for anyone—regardless of where they were. If the advice was followed, they got well. Newspapers throughout the country carried articles about his work, but it wasn't really until Gertrude was stricken with tuberculosis that the readings were brought home to him. Even with medical treatments she continued to grow worse and was not expected to live. Finally, the doctors said there was nothing more they could do. A reading was given and recommended such things as osteopathy, hydrotherapy, inhalants, dietary changes, and prescription medication. The advice was followed and Gertrude returned to perfectly normal health!

For decades, the Cayce readings have stood the test of time, research, and extensive study. Further details of Cayce's life and work are explored in such classic books as *There is a River* (1942) by Thomas Sugrue, *The Sleeping Prophet* (1967) by Jess Stearn, *Many Mansions* (1950) by Gina Cerminara, and *Edgar Cayce: An American Prophet* (2000) by Sidney Kirkpatrick.

Throughout his life, Edgar Cayce claimed no special abilities nor did he ever consider himself to be some kind of twentieth-century prophet. The readings never offered a set of beliefs that had to be embraced, but instead focused on the fact that each person should test in his or her own life the principles presented. Though Cayce himself was a Christian and read the Bible from cover to cover every year of his life, his work was one that stressed the importance of comparative study among belief systems all over the world. The underlying principle of the readings is the oneness of all life, a tolerance for all people, and a compassion and understanding for every major religion in the world.

Today, the Cayce organizations continue the legacy begun by Edgar Cayce with an undergirding mission to "help people change their lives for the better—physically, mentally, and spiritually—through the ideas in the Edgar Cayce material." Further information about Edgar Cayce's A.R.E., as well as activities, materials, and services, is available at EdgarCayce.org.

●

An Overview of Edgar Cayce on Creation and Evolution

Ever since the publication of Charles Darwin's *On the Origin of Species* in 1859 discussing the process of evolution by natural selection, there have been proponents on both sides of the argument challenging the "truths" of creationism versus evolution. The most conservative of Creationists have argued for a literal interpretation of the Bible, the creation of the earth in six days, and the all-pervading hand of God integrally involved in every aspect of the cosmos. The staunchest proponents of evolution describe the biological processes that make the involvement of a Creator unnecessary and describe a cosmos devoid of any Divine Intelligence. Obviously, there are individuals who find themselves somewhere in between, describing a creation that relies upon both a Creator and the evidentiary scientific laws of evolutionary processes. Edgar Cayce, the most documented psychic of all time, was one such individual—seeing both creation and evolution as ongoing universal forces shaping the cosmos and humankind. Although describing the importance of each, however, Cayce presents some unique ideas about the purpose of Creation and the ultimate end of evolution that may be challenging to proponents of both sides of the argument.

Since the dawn of time, Creation myths have existed around the world over as a means of explaining how the world came into being and how humankind became inhabitants of planet Earth. Over a period of forty-three years in hundreds of psychic readings, the Edgar Cayce material presented its own perspective of Creation and how humankind came to inhabit this planet. This vast wealth of information might be summarized as follows:

At the moment corresponding to what scientists have called "the Big Bang," a Divine Creator projected Creation from Himself. That creative spark moved into being the universe as well as souls that were given free will and the capacity to become like their Creator. For many millennia, these individual souls remained in tune with "spirit," watching much of the cosmos come into manifestation through the evolutionary processes that had been set in motion after the creative spark. In time, however, with their capacity for free will, some of the souls began to make choices that were out of accord with their divine nature.

Some of these curious souls came into the earth to watch the plant and animal kingdoms evolve, becoming fascinated by physical processes. Eventually, they became "trapped" in physicality and would be able to return only to their Divine awareness by perfectly manifesting "spirit" in the earth through a series of incarnations. Many thousands of years ago, one soul, whom the Cayce readings called "Amilius" decided to take upon himself the pattern for raising spiritual awareness in the earth. He was born into the earth as Adam and experienced a series of lifetimes before finally re-attaining spiritual perfection in the earth during His incarnation as Jesus. It is for this reason that the Cayce readings describe Jesus as the Elder Brother for all of humankind—a soul who showed the way to spiritual attainment regardless of one's religious background.

The readings also suggest that the souls first began projecting into the earth approximately 10 million years ago and that since then, two advanced civilizations had risen and fallen: a) the continent of Atlantis, which existed between 200,000 and 10,500 BC; and, b) an Egyptian civilization that predates (by many millennia) the timeline proposed by Egyptologists. Cayce's own readings suggest that he had been a part of this early Egyptian culture during an incarnation as Ra Ta—a high priest with a highly developed level of spiritual consciousness.

The readings also assert that creation and evolution are ongoing processes. Each soul is essentially a creative being and is constantly "creating" his or her life through thought, choice and action. In terms of evolution, the ultimate goal of evolution is "spiritual evolution" in that we might spiritually evolve to more fully become companions and co-creators with God. The readings suggest that there is also physical evolution *but* humanity did not descend from the monkey. Instead, the human creature was a unique form that was created with the capacity to perfectly manifest the divinity of the Creator in the earth.

In one remarkable reading (5749-14) given to Thomas Sugrue, the author of Cayce's biography, *There is a River*, questions were asked to provide a framework for the overarching philosophy and cosmology contained in the Cayce readings. Those questions included: a) the reason for Creation; b) the purpose for humankind's tenancy on earth; and, c) the role of Jesus as a pattern for all of humanity in terms of spiritual evolution.

In terms of Creation:

> (Q) The first problem concerns the reason for creation. Should this be given as God's desire to experience Himself, God's desire for companionship, God's desire for expression, or in some other way?
> (A) God's desire for companionship and expression.

In terms of humankind's tenancy on earth, the readings suggest that we are spiritual beings having a physical experience and that the "physical experience" was not necessarily required for our own spiritual evolution. However, once souls entered the environs of earth, they became subject to the universal laws governing same and would be required to reach "perfection" through a series of lifetimes in order to return to a full awareness of their spiritual essence:

> (Q) The third problem has to do with the fall of man. Should this be described as something which was inevitable in the destiny of souls, or something which God did not desire, but which He did not prevent once He had given free will? The problem here is to reconcile the omniscience of God and His knowledge of all things with the free will of the soul and the soul's fall from grace.
> (A) He did not prevent, once having given free will. For, He made the individual entities or souls in the beginning. For,

the beginnings of sin, of course, were in seeking expression of themselves outside of the plan or the way in which God had expressed same. Thus it was the individual, see? Having given free will, then—though having the foreknowledge, though being omnipotent and omnipresent—it is only when the soul that is a portion of God *chooses* that God knows the end thereof.
(Q) The fourth problem concerns man's tenancy on earth. Was it originally intended that souls remain out of earthly forms, and were the races originated as a necessity resulting from error?
(A) The earth and its manifestations were only the expression of God and not necessarily as a place of tenancy for the souls of men, until man was created—to meet the needs of existing conditions.

In terms of the role of Jesus as a pattern for humanity:

(Q) The ninth problem concerns the proper symbols, or similes, for the Master, the Christ. Should Jesus be described as the soul who first went through the cycle of earthly lives to attain perfection, including perfection in the planetary lives also?
(A) He should be. This is as the man, see?
(Q) Should this be described as a voluntary mission One Who was already perfected and returned to God, having accomplished His Oneness in other planes and systems?
(A) Correct.
(Q) Should the Christ-Consciousness be described as the awareness within each soul, imprinted in pattern on the mind and waiting to be awakened by the will, of the soul's oneness with God?
(A) Correct. That's the idea exactly!

The Edgar Cayce readings on creation and evolution are ultimately about the fact that we are spiritual beings having a physical experience. From this perspective, the main goal of earthly experience is to somehow bring "spirit" into the earth. Our collective purpose is to bring the very best we can conceive and imagine into the earth because we are children of a Divine creator charged with somehow manifesting divinity into the third dimension. That is why we are here. That is also the ultimate purpose for life. The means through which we can accomplish this incredible goal is through the universal processes of creation and evolution.

For Cayce, each individual is ultimately a companion and a co-creator with God. Creation is an ongoing process and every thought we think and every action we take has an impact upon that process. In terms of evolution, personal evolution is ultimately about correlating the human mind and soul toward perfection eventually becoming "at one" with the Divine Being who brought all of Creation into manifestation. In Cayce's terminology, it is about becoming "One with the oneness." It is our destiny to reawaken to the fact that we are spiritual beings manifesting in the earth.

Kevin J. Todeschi
Executive Director & CEO
Edgar Cayce's A.R.E. / Atlantic University

1

●

Creation/Atlantis Readings

Reading 3508-1

God moved, the spirit came into activity. In the moving it brought light, and then chaos. In this light came creation of that which in the earth came to be matter; in the spheres about the earth, space and time; and in patience it has evolved through those activities until there are the heavens and all the constellations, the stars, the universe as it is known—or sought to be known by individual soul-entities in the material plane.

Then came into the earth materiality, through the spirit pushing itself into matter. Spirit was individualized, and then became what we recognize in one another as individual entities. Spirit that uses matter, that uses every influence in the earth's environ for the glory of the Creative Forces, partakes of and is a part of the universal consciousness.

Reading 262-119

Just so have we seen and comprehended how that there is the Father, the Son, the Holy Spirit. The Spirit is the movement; as when God the First Cause—called into being *light* as a manifestation of the influences that would, through their movement (light movement) upon forces yet unseen, bring into being what we know as the universe—or matter; in all its forms, phases, manifestations.

1

Reading 262-99

When the earth became a dwelling place for matter, when gases formed into those things that man sees in nature and in activity about him, then matter began its ascent in the various forms of physical evolution—in the *mind* of God! The spirit chose to enter (celestial, not an earth spirit—he hadn't come into the earth yet!), chose to put on, to become a part of that which was as a command not to be done! Then those so entering *must* continue through the earth until the body-mind is made perfect for the soul, or the body-celestial again.

Reading 341-1

In the days before this we find the entity was among those in the day when the forces of the Universe came together, when there was upon the waters the sound of the coming together of the Sons of God, when the morning stars sang together, and over the face of the waters there was the voice of the glory of the coming of the plane for man's dwelling.

Reading 2497-1

In the one before this, we find in the beginning, when all forces were given in the spiritual force, and the morning stars sang together in the glory of the coming of the Lord and the God to make the giving of man's influence and developing in the world's forces.

Reading 294-8

. . . in the beginning, when the first of the elements were given, and the forces set in motion that brought about the sphere as we find called earth plane, and when the morning stars sang together, and the whispering winds brought the news of the coming of man's indwelling, of the spirit of the Creator, became the living soul. This entity came into being with this multitude.

Reading 364-10

From that which has been given, it is seen that individuals in the beginning were more of thought forms than individual entities with personalities as seen in the present, and their projections into the realms of fields of thought that pertain to a developing or evolving world of matter, with the varied presentations about same, of the expressions or attributes in the various things about the entity or individual, or body, through which such science—as termed now, or such phenomena as would be termed—became manifest. Hence we find occult or psychic science, as would be called at the present, was rather the natural state of man in the beginning. Very much as (in illustration) when a baby, or babe, is born into the world and its appetite is first satisfied, and it lies sleeping. Of what is its dreams? That it expects to be, or that it has been? Of what are thoughts? That which is to be, or that which has been, or that which is? Now remember we are speaking—these were thought forms, and we are finding again the illustrations of same!

. . . These, then, are the manners in which the *entities*, those *beings*, those *souls*, in the beginning partook of, or developed. Some brought about monstrosities, as those of its (that entity's) association by its projection with its association with beasts of various characters. Hence those of the Styx, satyr, and the like; those of the sea, or mermaid; those of the unicorn, and those of the various forms—these projections of what? The abilities in the *psychic* forces (psychic meaning, then, of the mental *and* the soul—doesn't necessarily mean the body, until it's enabled to be brought *into* being in whatever form it may make its manifestation—which may never be in a material world, or take form in a three-dimensional plane as the earth is; it may remain in a fourth-dimensional—which is an idea! Best definition that ever may be given of fourth-dimension is an idea! Where will it project? Anywhere! Where does it arise from? Who knows! Where will it end? Who can tell! It is all inclusive! It has both length, breadth, height and depth—is without beginning and is without ending! Dependent upon that which it may feed for its sustenance, or it may pass into that much as a thought or an idea. Now this isn't ideal that's said! It's idea! see?)

In the use of these, then, in this material plane—of these forces—brought about those that made for all *manners* of the various forms that are used in the material world today. *Many* of them to a much higher development. As those that sought forms of minerals—and being able to be that the mineral was, hence much more capable—in the psychic or occult force, or power—to classify, or make same in its own classifications. Who classified them? They were from the beginning! They are themselves! They were those necessities as were *in* the beginning from an *all wise* Creator! for remember these came, as did that as was to be the keeper of same! The husbandman of the vineyard! Each entity, each individual—today, has its own vineyard to keep, to dress—For who? Its Maker, from whence it came! What is to be the report in thine own life with those abilities, those forces, as may be manifest in self—through its calling upon, through what? How does prayer reach the throne of mercy or grace, or that from which it emanates? From itself! Through that of *crucifying, nullifying,* the carnal mind and opening the mental in such a manner that the Spirit of truth may flow in its psychic sense, or occult force, into the very being, that you may be one with that from which you came! Be thou faithful unto that committed into thy keeping! Life *itself* is precious! For why? It is of the Maker itself! That *is* the beginning! The psychic forces, the attunements, the developments, going *to* that! As did many in that experience. And Enoch walked with God, and he was not for God took him. As was many of those in those first years, in this land, this experience.

Reading 262–56

(Q) (General question) Please explain the existence of darkness before the existence of light.

(A) This has just been explained, to those who will read that given! That man, or war, or sin, or separation in glory of those that were heedless. Then, that there might be the way for those—What has been given as the most meaning of all that written? He has not willed that any soul should perish, but from the beginning has prepared a way of escape! What, then, is the meaning of the separation?

Bringing into being the various phases that the soul may find in its manifested forms the consciousness and awareness of its separation, and itself, by that through which it passes in all the various spheres of its awareness. Hence the separation, and light and darkness. Darkness, that it had separated—that a soul had separated itself from the light. Hence He called into being Light, that the awareness began. Hence we look out and see the heavens, the stars; and, as the psalmist has said: "The heavens declare the glory of God and the firmament sheweth his handiwork, as day unto day uttereth speech and night unto night sheweth knowledge."

(Q) Comment upon the following. Is it worthy of expansion; that is, does it carry any light of truth? The Creator, in seeking to find or create a being worthy of companionship, realized that such a being would result only from a free will exercising its divine inheritance and through its own efforts find its Maker. Thus, to make the choice really a Divine one caused the existence of states of consciousness, that would indeed tax the free will of a soul; thus light and darkness. Truly, only those tried so as by fire can enter in.

(A) The only variation that we would make is that all souls in the beginning were one with the Father. The separation, or turning away, brought evil. Then there became the necessity of the awareness of self's being out of accord with, or out of the realm of blessedness; and, as given of the Son, "yet learned he obedience through the things which he suffered."

Reading 281-42

As an illustration (this merely illustrating, now): It is hard for an individual, no matter how learned he may be, to conceive of the activities that exist only three miles above the earth. Why? Because there are no faculties within the individual entity in the present *capable* of conceiving that which is not represented within his individual self.

Yea—but the individual of that period was not so closely knit in matter. Thus the activities of the realms of relativity of force, relativity of attraction in the universe, *were* an experience of the souls manifesting in the earth at that period, see?

Thus we find that the experiences of individuals of the period, seeking for the understanding as to the evolution of the souls of men, might be compared to the minds of individuals in the present who are seeking an understanding as to man's use of physical or atomical structure in his own relationships.

Then, the individual of that experience or period was not necessarily one other than a soul or entity seeking the knowledge as to the relationship of that which would sustain and gain *for* man the abilities not only to continue the physical evolution but the spiritual or soul evolution as well.

Reading 518-1

Before that we find the entity was in the Atlantean land during those periods when there were the separations of the peoples from the

high and the low estates of the varied developments that were in that
period of man's experience in the earth, when there were the sons of
the High; or, as given in holy writ, "The Sons of God looked upon the
daughters of men."

The *entity* was among the sons of God, yet looking upon the daughters of men and making of self in those associations those periods when
faith was broken with others, and when there was the belittling of the
tenets and the truths in the *powers* that had been given among those
peoples for the manifesting of that which would cleanse their souls that
they might be one with the Creative Forces in this *material* world and
in the spiritual forces also.

Reading 294–189

For when the purposes of an entity or soul are the more and more in
accord with that for which the entity has entered, then the soul–entity
may take *hold* upon that which may bring to its remembrance that it
was, where, when and how. Thinkest thou that the grain of corn has
forgotten what manner of expression it has given?

Think thou that *any* of the influences in nature that you see about
you—the acorn, the oak, the elm, or the vine, or *anything*—has forgotten what manner of expression? Only man forgets! And it is only in
His mercy that such was brought about. For what was the first cause?
Knowledge—knowledge! What then is that cut off in the beginnings of
the Sons of God? Becoming entangled with the daughters of men, and
the Daughters of God becoming entangled with the sons of men! As
in Adam they forgot what manner of men they were! Only when he
lives, he manifests that life that is the expression of the divine, may man
begin to know *who*, where, what and when he was! That there may be
read from the records of God's Book of Remembrance, as from here, in
the keepers of the records, is true—if thy purpose, thy desire, in heart,
in soul, is for the love of God as may be manifested among the sons
of men; but these may read only by those in the shadows of His love.

Reading 262–119

(Q) Explain the "Sons of God—Daughters of Men—Sons of Man."
(A) This, too, has been given again and again. As has been indicated
through other associations, the influences of those souls that sought

material expression pushed themselves into thought forms in the earth. And owing to the earth's relative position with the activities in this particular sphere of activity in the universe, it was chosen as the place for expression. *Think*—universe, eternity, time, space! What do these mean to the finite mind? More often than otherwise they are just names. More often we think of spirit as just a name, rather than experiencing it. Yet we use it, we manifest it, we are a part of it. Taking *thought* doesn't change anything! It is the application of the thought taken that makes the change within ourselves! Then, as those expressed they were called the Sons of the Earth or Sons of Man.

When the Creative Forces, God, made then the first man—or Godman—he was the beginning of the Sons of God. Then those souls who entered through a channel made by God—not by thought, not by desire, not by lust, not by things that separated continually—were the Sons of God, the Daughters of God.

The Daughters of Men, then, were those who became the channels through which lust knew its activity; and it was in this manner then that the conditions were expressed as given of old, that the Sons of God looked upon the Daughters of Men and saw that they were fair, and *lusted!* What did the Christ say? "Ye say in the law that ye shall not commit adultery. I say unto you, he that looketh on a woman to *lust* after her hath committed adultery already!" Understandest thou? Then, what did it mean? Only that such channels offered ways and means for the expression of those influences claimed by Satan, the Devil, the Evil One, as his. But *He*, the only begotten of the Father, the Christ, has become the Way, the Light, the Truth, the Water, the Bread, the Vine! and all of those are *of* Him who become channels for manifesting, or through which there may be those expressions that are of love and faith and hope! Hence the two influences that are ever before thee; good and evil, life and death; choose thou!

Reading 257–201

For that is the purpose of the soul's being in the beginning. Hence without beginning, without end.

Hence as we find, when souls sought or found manifestation in materiality by the projection of themselves into matter—as became thought forms—and when this had so enticed the companions or souls of the Creator, first we had then the creation in which "God breathed into man (God-made) the breath of life and he became a living soul," with the abilities to become godlike.

Hence we find the first preparation or estate, or manner in which those souls might through material manifestation acclaim—by the living, by the being—that which was and is and ever will be consistent with the purposes of creation—was given into the estate of man. [Atlantis?]

The entity was among those first who through those channels came into consciousness, awareness of the relationships of the material man to the Creative Forces; that came into material activity during the early portions of man's *consciousness* of being an independent entity, or body, in a material existence. [Atlantis?]

Reading 364-3

The position as the continent Atlantis occupied, is that as between the Gulf of Mexico on the one hand—and the Mediterranean upon the other. Evidences of this lost civilization are to be found in the Pyrenees and Morocco on the one hand, British Honduras, Yucatan and America upon the other. There are some protruding portions within this that must have at one time or another been a portion of this great continent. The British West Indies or the Bahamas, and a portion of same that may be seen in the present—if the geological survey would be made in some of these—especially, or notably, in Bimini and in the Gulf Stream through this vicinity, these may be even yet determined.

What, then, are the character of the peoples? To give any proper conception, may we follow the line of a group, or an individual line, through this continent's existence—and gain from same something of their character, their physiognomy, and their spiritual and physical development.

In the period, then—some hundred, some ninety-eight thousand years before the entry of Ram into India—there lived in this land of Atlantis one Amilius [?], who had first *noted* that of the separations of the beings as inhabited that portion of the earth's sphere or plane of those peoples into male and female as separate entities, or individuals. As to their forms in the physical sense, these were much *rather* of the nature of *thought forms*, or able to push out *of themselves* in that direction in which its development took shape in thought—much in the way and manner as the amoeba would in the waters of a stagnant bay, or lake, in the present. As these took form, by the gratifying of their own desire for that as builded or added to the material conditions, they became hardened or set—much in the form of the existent human body of the day, with that of color as partook of its surroundings much in the manner as the chameleon in the present. Hence coming into that form as the red, or the mixture peoples—or colors; known then later by the associations as the *red* race. These, then, able to use *in* their gradual development all the forces as were manifest in their individual surroundings, passing through those periods of developments as has been followed more closely in that of the yellow, the black, or the white races, in other portions of the world; yet with their immediate surroundings, with the facilities for the developments, these became much speedier in this particular portion of the globe than in others—and while the destruction of this continent and the peoples are far beyond any of that as has been kept as an absolute record, that record in the rocks still remains—as has that influence *of* those peoples in that life of those peoples to whom those that did escape during the periods of destruction make or influence the lives of those peoples *to* whom they came. As they *may* in the present, either through the direct influence of being regenerated, or re-incarnated into the earth, or through that of the *mental* application on through the influences as may be had upon thought *of* individuals or groups by speaking from that environ.

In the *manner* of living, in the manner of the moral, of the social, of the religious life of these peoples: There, classes existed much in the same order as existed among others; yet the like of the warlike *influence* did *not* exist in the peoples—*as* a people—as it did in the *other* portions of the universe.

Reading 262–57

(Q) Please explain the statement given in Genesis, "In six days God made the heaven and the earth and *rested the seventh day.*"

(A) That each may interpret this to his own comprehension is rather that each becomes aware of the power of the Father in His manifestations in the earth. When it is considered (as was later given, or *written* even before this was written) that "a thousand years is as but a day and a day as but a thousand years in the sight of the Lord," then it may be comprehended that this was colored by the writer in his desire to express to the people the power of the living God—rather than a statement of six days as man comprehends days in the present. Not that it was an impossibility—but rather that men under the environ should be impressed by the omnipotence of that they were called on to worship as God.

Reading 5748-1

Yes, we have the work here and that phase concerning the indwelling in the earth's plane of those who first gave laws concerning indwelling of Higher Forces in man. In giving such in an understandable manner to man of today, [it is] necessary that the conditions of the earth's surface and the position of man in the earth's plane be understood, for the change has come often since this period, era, age, of man's earthly indwelling, for then at that period, only the lands now known as the Sahara and the Nile region appeared on the now African shores; that in Tibet, Mongolia, Caucasia and Norway in Asia and Europe; that in the southern cordilleras and Peru in the southwestern hemisphere and the plane of now Utah, Arizona, Mexico of the north-western hemisphere, and the spheres were then in the latitudes much as are presented at the present time.

The man's indwelling [was] then in the Sahara and the upper Nile regions, the waters then entering the now Atlantic from the Nile region rather than flowing northward. The waters in the Tibet and Caucasian entering the North Sea, those in Mongolia entering the South Seas, those in the cordilleras entering the Pacific, those in the plateau entering the Northern Seas.

When the earth brought forth the seed in her season, and man came in the earth plane as the lord of that in that sphere, man appeared in five places then at once—the five senses, the five reasons, the five spheres, the five developments, the five nations.

Reading 900-227

The earth and the universe, as related to man, came into being through the *mind—mind*—of the Maker, and, as such, has its same being much as each atomic force multiplies in itself, or, as worlds are seen and being made in the present period, and as same became (earth we are speaking of) an abode for man, man entered as man, through the *mind* of the Maker, see? in the form of flesh *man*; that which carnally might die, decay, become dust, entering into material conditions. The Spirit the gift of God, that man might be One with Him, with the concept of man's creative forces throughout the physical world. Man, in Adam (as a group; not as an individual), entered into the world (for he entered in five places at once, we see—called Adam in one, see?), and as man's concept became to that point wherein man walked not after the ways of the Spirit but after the desires of the flesh *sin* entered—that is, away from the Face of the Maker, see? and death then became man's portion, *spiritually*, see? for the physical death existed from the beginning; for to create one must die, see? In this, then, there is seen, as the body, in the flesh, of the Christ, became perfect in the flesh, in the world, and the body laid aside on the Cross, in the tomb, the *physical* body moved away, through that as *man* will know as dimensions, and the Spirit able then to take hold of that Being in the way as it enters again into the body, and as it presents itself to the world, to individuals at the time and to man at present.

Reading 364–9

(Q) Was Atlantis one of the five points at which man appeared in the beginning, being the home of the red race?

(A) One of the five points. As has been given, in what is known as Gobi, India, in Carpathia [?], or in that known as the Andes, and that known as in the western plain of what is now called America—the five places. In their presentation, as we find, these—in the five places, as *man* (Let's get the difference in that as first appeared in what is known as Atlantis, and that as *man* appearing from those projections in the five places—and, as has been given, from their environ took on that as became necessary for the meeting of those varying conditions under which their individualities and personalities began to put on form)— one in the white, another in the brown, another in the black, another in the red. These, as we find, taking that form—Would snow be the place for the black? or the sun the place for the white? or the desert and the hills for either the white or black? as were partakers of those things that brought about those variations in that which enters, or becomes as the outer presentation, or the skin, or the pigment that is presented in same.

Reading 364–7

GC: You will have before you the material, or information, given through this channel on the Lost Continent of Atlantis, a copy of which I hold in my hand. You will answer the questions which I will ask regarding this:

EC: Yes, we have the information as has been transcribed here. Ready for questions.

(Q) How is the legend of Lilith connected with the period of Amilius?

(A) In the beginning, as was outlined, there was presented that that became as the Sons of God, in that male and female were as one, with those abilities for those changes as were able or capable of being brought about. In the changes that came from those *things*, as were of the projections of the abilities of those entities to project, this as a being came as the companion; and when there was that turning to the within, through the sources of creation, as to make for the helpmeet of that as created by the first cause, or of the Creative Forces that brought into being that as was made, *then*—from out of self—was brought that as was to be the helpmeet, *not* just companion of the body. Hence the legend of the associations of the body during that period before there was brought into being the last of the creations, which was not of that that was *not* made, but the first of that that *was* made, and a helpmeet to the body, that there might be no change in the relationship of the *sons* of God *with* those relationships of the sons and daughters of men. In this then, also comes that as is held by many who have reached especially to that understanding of how *necessary*, then, becomes the *proper* mating of those souls that may be the *answers* one to another of that that may bring, through that association, that companionship, into being that that may be the more helpful, more sustaining, more the well-*rounded* life or experience of those that are a *portion* one of another. Do not misinterpret, but knowing that all are *of* one—yet there are those divisions that make for a *closer* union, when there are the proper relationships brought about. As an illustration, in this: In the material world we find there is in the mineral kingdom those elements that are of the nature as to form a closer union one with another, and make as for compounds as make for elements that act more in unison with, or against, other forms of activity in the experience in the earth's environ, or the earth's force, as makes for those active forces in the *elements* that are *about* the earth. Such as we may find in those that make for the active forces in that of uranium, and that of ultramarine, and these make then for an element that becomes the more active force as with the abilities for the rates of emanation as may be thrown off from same. So, as illustrated in the union, then, of—in the *physical* compounds—that as may vibrate, or make for emanations in the activities of their mental and spiritual, and material, or physical forces, as may make for a *greater* activity in this earth environ. Then, there may be seen that as is in an elemental, or compound, that makes for that as is seen in the material experience as to become an antipathy for other elements that are as equally necessary in the experience of man's environ as in the combination of gases as may produce whenever combined that called water, and its antipathy for the elements in combustion is easily seen or known in man's experience. So in those unions of that in the elemental forces of creative energies that take on the form of man, either in that of man or woman, with its *natural* or *elemental*, see? *elemental* forces of its vibration, with the union of two that vibrate or respond to those vibrations in self, create for that ideal that becomes as that, in that created, in the form—as is known as radium, with its fast emittal vibrations, that brings for active forces, principles, that makes for such atomic forces within the active principles of all nature in its active force as to be one of the elemental bases from which life in its essence, as an active principle in a material world, has its sources, give off that which is *ever* good—unless abused, see? So in that may there be basis for *those* forces, as *has* been, as *is* sought, thought, or *attained by* those who have, through the abilities of the vibrations, to make for a continued force in self as to meet, know, see, feel, understand, those sources from which such begets that of its kind, or as those that become as an antipathy for another, or as makes for those that makes for the variations in the tempering of the various elements, compounds, or the like; so, as is seen, *these*—then—the *basis* for those things as has been given here, there, in their various ways and manners, as to the companion of, and *companions* of, that that first able—through its projection of itself and its abilities in the creation—to bring about that that was either of its *own* making, or creation, or that given in the beginning to *be* the force *through* which there might *be* that that would bring ever blessings, good, right, and love, in even the physical or material world. See?

(Q) How long did it take for the division into male and female?

(A) That depends upon which, or what branch or *line* is considered. When there was brought into being that as of the projection of that created *by* that created, this took a period of evolutionary—or, as would be in the present year, fourscore and six year. That as brought into being as was of the creating *of* that that became a portion of, *of* that that was already created by the *creator, that* brought into being as *were* those of the forces of nature itself. God said, "Let there be light" and there *was* light! God said, "Let there be life" and there *was* life!

(Q) Were the thought forms that were able to push themselves out of themselves inhabited by souls, or were they of the animal kingdom?

(A) That as created by that *created*, of the animal kingdom. That created as by the Creator, with the soul...

(Q) Please give the important re-incarnations of Adam in the world's history.

(A) In the beginning as Amilius, as Adam, as Melchizedek, as Zend [?], as Ur [?] [Enoch? GD's note: Perhaps Ur was prehistory person [364-9, Par. 3-A] who established Ur of the Chaldees? I don't think he was mentioned anywhere else in the readings as an incarnation of Jesus.], as Asaph [?] [Songs of Asaph? See Ps. 81:5 indicating that Joseph and Asaph were one and the same?], as Jesus [Jeshua]—Joseph—Jesus. [See 364-9, Par. 3-A.] Then, as that coming into the world in the second coming—for He will come again and receive His own, who have prepared themselves through that belief in Him and acting in that manner; for the *spirit* is abroad, and the time draws near, and there will be the reckoning of those even as in the first so in the last, and the last shall be first; for there is that Spirit abroad—He standeth near. He that hath eyes to see, let him see. He that hath ears to hear, let him hear that music of the coming of the Lord of this vineyard, and art *thou* ready to give account of that *thou* hast done with thine opportunity in the earth as the Sons of God, as the heirs and joint heirs of glory *with* the Son? Then make thine paths straight, for there must come an answering for that *thou* hast done with thine Lord! He will not tarry, for having overcome He shall appear even *as* the Lord *and* Master. Not as one born, but as one that returneth to His own, for He will walk and talk with men of every clime, and those that are faithful and just in their reckoning shall be caught up with Him to rule and to do judgment for a thousand years!

Reading 364–6

(Q) How large was Atlantis during the time of Amilius?

(A) Comparison, that of Europe including Asia in Europe—not Asia, but Asia in Europe—see? This composed, as seen, in or after the first of the destructions, that which would be termed now—with the present position—the southernmost portion of same—islands as created by those of the first (as man would call) volcanic or eruptive forces brought into play in the destruction of same.

(Q) Was Atlantis one large continent, or a group of large islands?

(A) Would it not be well to read just that given? Why confuse in the questionings? As has been given, what would be considered one large continent, until the first eruptions brought those changes—from what would now, with the present position of the earth in its rotation, or movements about its sun, through space, about Arcturus, about the Pleiades, that of a whole or one continent. Then with the breaking up, producing more of the nature of large islands, with the intervening canals or ravines, gulfs, bays or streams, as came from the various *elemental* forces that were set in motion by this *charging*—as it were—*of* the forces that were collected as the basis for those elements that would produce destructive forces, as might be placed in various quarters or gathering places of those beasts, or the periods when the larger animals roved the earth—*with* that period of man's indwelling. Let it be remembered, or not confused, that the *earth* was peopled by *animals* before peopled by man! First that of a mass, which there arose the mist, and then the rising of same with light breaking *over* that as it *settled* itself, as a companion of those in the universe, as it began its *natural* (or now natural) rotations, with the varied effects *upon* the various portions of same, as it slowly—and is slowly—receding or gathering closer to the sun, from which it receives its impetus for the awakening of the elements that give life itself, by radiation of like elements from that which it receives from the sun. Hence that of one type, that has been through the ages, of mind—that gives the *sun* as the father *of* light in the earth. Elements have their attraction and detraction, or those of *animosity* and those of gathering together. This we see throughout all of the kingdoms, as may be termed, whether we speak of the heavenly hosts or of those of the stars, or of the planets, or of the various forces within any or all of same, they have their attraction or detraction. The attraction increases that as gives an impulse, that that becomes the aid, the stimuli, or an impulse to create. Hence, as may be seen—or may be brought to man's own—that of attraction one for another gives that *stimuli*, that *impulse*, to be the criterion of, or the gratification of, those influences in the experience of individuals or entities. To smother same oft becomes deteriorations for each other, as may come about in any form, way or manner. Accidents happen in creation, as well as in individuals' lives! Peculiar statement here, but—true!

Reading 364-13

(Q) Are the places designated for the beginning of the five races correct?

(A) As we find, these are changed, in that: Those in the Gobi, the yellow. The white—rather in the Carpathians than India, though this is the change to which they are made. The red, of course, in the Atlantean and in the American. The brown in the Andean. The black in the plain and the Sudan, or in African.

(Q) Where was the Carpathian region?

(A) Aarat.

(Q) Where is the location? Is it on the map today?

(A) Southern part of Europe and Russia, and Persia and that land. Caucasian mountains.

(Q) Why was the number five selected for the projection of the five races?

(A) This, as we find, is that element which represents man in his physical form, and the attributes to which he may become conscious *from* the elemental or spiritual to the physical consciousness. As the senses; as the sensing *of* the various forces that bring to man the activities in the sphere in which he finds himself. This, to be sure, may be expanded upon. This must bear in the same relation to that as did exist, to the promise that He will come again. Does any individual group think of themselves so exalted as that only to one peoples will He appear as in the beginning, so shall it ever be, that man's indwelling must recognize that not only must his desires carnally be crucified, but all elements that make for the awareness *of* the spiritual manifestations in the material plane!

(Q) Did the appearance of what became the five races occur simultaneously?

(A) Occurred at once.

(Q) Describe the earth's surface at the period of the appearance of the five projections.

(A) This has been given. In the first, or that known as the beginning, or in the Caucasian and Carpathian, or the Garden of Eden, in that land which lies now much in the desert, yet much in mountain and much in the rolling lands there. The extreme northern portions were then the southern portions, or the polar regions were then turned to where they occupied more of the tropical and semi-tropical regions; hence it would be hard to discern or disseminate the change. The Nile entered into the Atlantic Ocean. What is now the Sahara was an inhabited land and very fertile. What is now the central portion of this country, or the Mississippi basin, was then all in the ocean; only the plateau was existent, or the regions that are now portions of Nevada, Utah and Arizona formed the greater part of what we know as the United States. That along the Atlantic board formed the outer portion then, or the lowlands of Atlantis. The Andean, or the Pacific coast of South America, occupied then the extreme western portion of Lemuria. The Urals and the northern regions of same were turned into a tropical land. The desert in the Mongolian land was then the fertile portion. This may enable you to form *some* concept of the status of the earth's representations at that time! The oceans were then turned about; they no longer bear their names, yet from whence obtained they their names? What is the legend, even, as to their names?

(Q) Are the following the correct places? Atlantean, the red.

(A) Atlantean and American, the red race.

(Q) Upper Africa for the black?

(A) Or what would be known now as the more *western* portion of upper Egypt for the black. You see, with the changes—when there came the uprisings in the Atlantean land, and the sojourning southward—with the turning of the axis, the white and yellow races came more into that portion of Egypt, India, Persia and Arabia.

(Q) There was no original projection in upper India?

(A) This was a portion rather of the white and the yellow as repre-

sented. Let these represent the attributes of the physical, or the senses and what forms they take, rather than calling them white, black,
yellow, red and green, etc. What do they signify in the *sensing*? Sight,
vision—white. Feeling—red. Black—gratifying of appetites in the senses.
Yellow—mingling in the hearing. What is the law of the peoples that
these represent? Their basic thoughts run to those elements!

Reading 364-11
(Q) Please give a few details regarding the physiognomy, habits,
customs and costumes of the people of Atlantis during the period just
before this first destruction.
(A) These, as we find, will require their being separated in the gradual
development of the body and its physiognomy as it came into being in
the various portions of that land, as well as to those that would separate themselves from those peoples where there were the indwelling of
peoples, or man—as man, in the various areas of the land, or what we
call world. In the matter of form, as we find, first there were those as
projections from that about the animal kingdom; for the *thought* bodies
gradually took form, and the various *combinations* (as may be called) of
the various forces that called or classified themselves as gods, or rulers
over—whether herds, or fowls, or fishes, etc.—in *part* that kingdom and
part of that as gradually evolved into a physiognomy much in the form
of the present day may (were one chosen of those that were, or are, the
nearest representative of the race of peoples that existed in this first
period as the first destructions came about). These took on *many* sizes
as to stature, from that as may be called the midget to the giants—for
there were giants in the earth in those days, men as tall as (what would
be termed today) ten to twelve feet in stature, and in proportion—well
proportioned throughout. The ones that became the most *useful* were
those as would be classified (or called in the present) as the *ideal* stature, that was of both male and female (as those separations had been
begun); and the most ideal (as would be called) was Adam, who was in
that period when he (Adam) appeared as five in one—See? In this the
physiognomy was that of a full head, with an extra *eye*—as it were—in
those portions that became what is known as the *eye*. In the beginning
these appeared in *whatever* portion was desired by the body for its use!
As for the dress, those in the beginning were (and the Lord made for

them coats) of the skins of the animals. These covered the parts of their person that had become, then, as those portions of their physiognomy that had brought much of the desires that made for destructive forces in their own experience; and these then were of those *about* them that were given as meat, or used as same—that partook of the herbs. These were those same herbs that the seed were to have been for food for the man in self, and only those that partook of same may be called even *clean*—in the present day. Those that supply those same materials that are the proper building for the forces within the anatomical forces, or physiological forces, of a developing body; for these carry all the elements in their natural state. Little of minerals should ever be the properties within the system, save as may be taken through the vegetable forces, save where individuals have so laxed themselves as to require or need that which will make for an even balance of same.

Reading 364-5

(Q) Explain the information given regarding Amilius [?], who first noted the separation of the peoples into male and female, as it relates to the story in the Bible of Adam and Eve, in the Garden of Eden giving the name of the symbols Adam, Eve, the apple, and the serpent.

(A) This would require a whole period of a lecture period for this alone; for, as is seen, that as is given is the presentation of a teacher of a peoples that separated for that definite purpose of keeping alive in the minds, the hearts, the *soul* minds of entities, that there may be seen their closer relationship to the divine influences of Creative Forces, that brought into being all that appertains to man's indwelling as man in the form of flesh in this material world. These are presented in symbols of that thought as held by those peoples from whom the physical recorder took those records as compiled, with that gained by himself in and through the entering into that state where the entity's soul mind drew upon the records that are made by the passing of time itself in a material world. As given, these are records not only of the nature as has been termed or called akashic records (that is, of a mental or soul record), but that in a more material nature as set down in stone, that was attempted to be done—*has* been attempted to be done throughout *all* time! *Why* does man *now* set in stone those that are representatives of that desired to be kept in mind by those making records for future generations? There are many more materials more lasting, as is known to many. In the records, then, as this: There are, as seen, the records made by the man in the mount, that this Amilius [?]—Adam, as given— first discerned that from himself, not of the beasts about him, could be drawn—*was* drawn—that which made for the propagation *of* beings *in* the flesh, that made for that companionship as seen by creation in the material worlds about same. The story, the tale (if chosen to be called such), is one and the same. The apple, as 'the apple of the eye', the desire of that companionship innate in that created, as innate in the Creator, that brought companionship into the creation itself. Get that one! In this there comes, then, that which is set before that created—or having *taken on* that form, able of projecting itself in *whatever* direction it chose to take, as given; able to make itself *of* that environ, in color, in harmony, in *whatever* source that makes for the spirit of that man would attempt to project in music, in art, in *any* form that may even be conceivable to the mind itself in what may be termed its most lucid moments, in its most esoteric moments, in its highest animation moments; for were He not the *son* of the living God made manifest, that He might be the companion in a made world, in material manifested things, with the injunction to subdue all, *bring* all in the material things under subjection—all *under* subjection—by that ability to project itself *in* its way? *knowing* itself, as given, to be a portion *of* the whole, in, through, of, by the whole? In this desire, then, keep—as the injunction was—thine self separate: *of* that seen, but *not* that seen. The apple, then, that desire for that which made for the associations that bring carnal-minded influences of that brought as sex influence, known in a material world, and the partaking of same is that which brought the influence in the lives of that in the symbol of the serpent, that made for that which creates the desire that may be only satisfied in gratification of carnal forces, as partake of the world and its influences about same—rather than of the spiritual emanations from which it has its source. Will control—inability of will control, if we may put it in common parlance.

Reading 281-44

(Q) What is meant by automatons who labored in that experience? Were they individual souls developing, or was it spiritual evolution?

(A) Both, and neither. They were the offspring of the Sons of God with the Daughters of Men, or vice versa.

Reading 137–12

(Q) It is given in the horoscope reading, the entity's first appearance on earth was when the Sons of God came together to reason in the elements as to the appearance of man in physical on earth's plane. Explain what is meant by the Sons of God and how they came to reason about man's appearance on earth.

(A) In the evolution of those conditions relating to the development upon earth's plane, and the time came for the dwelling of man in physical forces, the Sons of God came together. As is given, in the beginning was the Word, and the Word *was* God. The same was in the beginning. All those forces that, co-related, make the Universal Forces in the spheres about the earth were brought together, as in one. This entity, in its present earth plane, one among that sphere, and able in the present sphere (earth plane) to co-relate through that Divine in the entity to manifest such conditions in an earth plane. As this force, then, became manifested in the earth's forces (material forces), this entity became one manifest in the flesh, presently known in flesh as [137]. These conditions, as we find, come with those relative forces of the spirit manifest in the spirit.

2

●

Evolution

Reading 1479–1

For it is ever, in the evolution of man in materiality, here a little, there a little, line upon line, precept upon precept. For He is mindful and hath not willed that any soul should perish, but has with every affliction, with every disturbance, with every disappointment prepared a way, a means for a helpful experience, if the entity, the soul, will but look up, *lift* up the eyes to the hill—yea to the tabernacle within self—for that healing that comes to every heart, every soul.

Reading 3189–2

In analyzing the urges that have prompted the individual entity many things or conditions enter therein. The premise from which this information is drawn as it is a part of the record upon time, is that very influence as related one to another, even as man in the elements of the body is of the earth-earthy. For, it was made from that which was already a part of God's evolution. Thus the physical body is oft subject to those things and influences, those related things. Thus in the physical body radiation, water and mind urge, play an important part. The entity may thus so raise the consciousness of the mental and spiritual self as has been the experience at times of this entity, to "put away" or overcome those influences that may have been about the urge. For, the law of the Lord is perfect, converting the soul. This is truly applicable here.

Reading 2271–1

For, the experience or sojourn in the earth is not by chance, but the natural spiritual and soul evolution of the entity; that it may be aware of its relationships to God—through its relationships to its fellow men; recognizing in each soul, as well as in self, those possibilities, those opportunities, those duties, those obligations that are a portion of each soul-entity's manifesting in a material plane.

Reading 3744–5

(Q) Definition of the word evolution with reference to the human family:

(A) Evolution with reference to the human family. Evolution is, as commonly understood by the human family, and upon which there has been much discussion by many peoples, and the question has become one that involves many different phases and meanings to many peoples. Evolution is as reference. In reference to the human family, means rather resuscitation of those forces that have gradually brought man to understand the law of self from within, and by understanding such law has brought the better force in man to bring about the gradual change that has come to man, known through all the ages.

Man was made as man. There was, there is, as we find, only three of the creations as is given, matter, force and mind. In each we find that, in the forces as is developed into the conditions, as we find at the present time. All flesh is not of one flesh, but the developing of one has always remained in the same, and has only been to meet the needs of man, for which there was made all that was made, and man's evolving, or evolution, has only been that of the gradual growth upward to the mind of the Maker.

(Q) Is the Darwinian theory of evolution of man right or wrong? Give such an answer as will enlighten the people on this subject of evolution.

(A) Man was made in the beginning, as the ruler over those elements as was prepared in the earth plane for his needs. When the plane became that such as man was capable of being sustained by the forces, and conditions, as were upon the face of the earth plane, man appeared not from that already created, but as the Lord over all that was created, and in man there is found that in the living man, all of that, that may be found without in the whole, whole world or earth plane, and *other* than that, the *soul of man* is that making him above all animal, vegetable, mineral kingdom of the earth plane.

Man *did not* descend from the monkey, but man has evolved, resuscitation, you see, from time to time, time to time, here a little, there a little, line upon line and line upon line. In all ages we find this has been the developing—day by day, day by day, or the evolution as we see from those forces as may be manifested by that, that man has made himself the gradual improvement upon the things made by man, yet made to suffice the needs of certain functioning portions of man's will force, as may be manifested by man, but ever remaining that element to supply that need, whether of sustenance or other functions of man's individual needs, as created by man, this becoming then the exponent of the force as his Creator made him, for the World, and the needs and conditions, man's compliance nearer with those laws brings him gradually to that development necessary to meet the needs of the conditions, place or sphere in which that individual is placed. As in this:

The needs of those in the North Country not the same as those in the Torrid region. Hence development comes to meet the needs in the various conditions under which man is placed. He only using those laws that are ever and ever in existence in the plane, as is given in that of relativity, that being the needs from one relation to another.

The theory is, man evolved, or evolution, from first cause in creation, and brings forth to meet the needs of the man, the preparation for the needs of man has gone down many, many thousands and millions of years, as is known in this plane, for the needs of man in the hundreds and thousands of years to come. Man is man, and God's order of creation, which he represents even as His son, who is the representative of the Father, took on the form of Man, the highest of the creation in the plane, and became to man that element that shows and would show and will show the way, the directing way, the Life, the Water, the Vine, to the everlasting, when guided and kept in that manner and form.

(Q) Where does the soul come from, and how does it enter the physical body?

(A) It is already there. " . . . and He breathed into him the breath of life, and he became a living soul," as the breath, the ether from the forces as come into the body of the human when born breathes the breath of life, as it becomes a living soul, provided it has reached that developing in the creation where the soul may enter and find the lodging place. All souls were created in the beginning, and are finding their way back to whence they came.

(Q) Where does the soul go when fully developed?

(A) To its Maker.

Reading 254–95

. . . for time and space are as the evolution upon which the forces of the divine make for that change that brings same into the experiences of those souls who seek to become one with the Creative Energies. Hence *all* may be touched, *all* may be drawn upon. And, as has been given, if it were individualized by a guide, it would become limited; while if universal it is in the hands of Him that is the Maker, the Giver, the Creator. For hath He not given, "Abide in me, as I in the Father, that I in the Father may be glorified in thee!" Ye that seek self-glory know its hardships. Ye that seek the glory of the Father know its beauties.

Reading 900–70

(Q) Explain as clearly as possible the definition of Evolution as relates to Man, first in Spirit plane, then in flesh and blood on earth and again in spirit plane. What is man and how may we in flesh become fully conscious and aware of the Spiritual Self?

(A) In this we find the understanding would, from physical viewpoint, never be understood by the cycle as is asked. The evolution of man in spiritual plane being one, the evolution of man in flesh being another. Hence, as has been given, hard to understand conditions in one plane when viewed from another plane, without the realization of having experienced that plane. Now evolution in flesh, as is seen, is the passing through the flesh plane and in the various experiences of man's sojourn in earth, through his (man's) environment as created and made by man, this is called man's evolution in the earth plane. As we have in the beginning of man's sojourn in earth plane, we find under what is termed at the present time or day, or plane of man, the primitive man. The man seeking the first of the attributes of fleshly existence, known only by those conditions surrounding man and his environments. As man applies the laws of which he (man) becomes conscious of, the development of man brings forth those results merited by that knowledge. As man passes into the spiritual plane from earthly existence, the development in the spiritual plane becoming the same evolution in spiritual planes as is acquired in the physical plane, and until man becomes in the spiritual sense the one-ness with the Creator's forces, as is set by example of the Son of Man coming in the flesh to the earth plane to manifest in the flesh the will made one with the Father, passing through the physical plane, passing through the spiritual planes, making *all* one with the Father. This we find then is evolution. Man's development through man's acquiring man's understanding of spiritual laws, of earthly laws, of God's laws, and applying same in the earth. Then truly is it given, "The righteous shall inherit the earth."

(Q) Does Man created as Matter, Force and Mind mean Physical, Spiritual and Mental?

A) Man created having the attributes of the physical, the spiritual, the mental, to work with in his own development. These, as it were, tools of the whole man, the all being then one, and that same separated is the attributes of the various conditions, each having its single, its separate attributes, and man using same for man's development.

(Q) When Earth Plane became ready for Man, how did he first get here? In the Bible we have the story of Adam and Eve. Explain in a reasonable, logical way how did Man first appear on Earth. Explain this in relation to birth, to conception.

(A) As is given, man, when earth became habitable for physical man, man entered in the plane, just as the highest of created forces in the earth plane. Then became man amenable to laws of earth plane, and amenable to physical birth, physical conditions, physical conceptions, physical forces as applied to the whole man. Physical, mental and spiritual forces manifest in man, taken in this conception as was given from the beginning. As the earth plane became in that state wherein man may find residence, the spirit forces as are developing through the spiritual forces to make one with the Father, given the soul of man to make manifest in the flesh. All souls were created in the beginning, all spirit of one spirit, Spirit of God, that spirit manifest in flesh, that spirit manifest in all creation, whether of earthly forces or Universal forces, all spirit being one spirit. All flesh not one flesh. Flesh being that as has merited by its development in its plane of existence.

(Q) Is every chemical quality found in the animal, vegetable and mineral kingdom of the world found in Man? Explain, if not, what is meant by "There is found in Living Man all of that that may be found without in the whole world".

(A) All those essential forces as are manifest in the Universe is manifest in the living man, and above that the soul of man. The chemical or material, or animated forces as are seen in all animal, vegetable, mineral forces, with their combinations, are found in the combinations in man, and from same may be created, for man is Lord over creation, from the physical viewpoint.

(Q) Explain how the example of Man's developing and improving his mode of living scientifically on earth, for example in medical work and all other sciences, proves his development and evolution on earth and other planes.

(A) Man's development, as given, is of man's understanding and applying the laws of the Universe, and as man applies those, man develops, man brings up the whole generation of man. Individuals we find carry out certain elements and laws, and gradually man becomes capable of applying and using those in the everyday life of man. This, whether applied in medical science, in anatomal science, in mechanical science or what not, is merely the development, or the application as man applies to Universal laws as are ever, and have ever been, existent in the Universe. As is in this. That producing electrical units of force was just as applicable to the Universal forces in the days of Adam as in the days of the Master, or as in the days of to-day. Those laws applying to aerial of transmission just as applicable in one as in other. Man not understanding those. Many times has the evolution of the earth reached the stage of development as it has to-day and then sank again, to rise again in the next development. Some along one line, some along others, for often we find the higher branches of so-called learning destroys itself in the seed it produces in man's development, as we have in medical forces, as we have astrological forces, as we have in some forms of spiritual forces, as we have in forms of destructive forces of the various natures.

(Q) Explain how the law of Relativity applies to Man's development to his evolution?

(A) As each and every atom in the Universe has its relative relation with every other atom, then man's development lies in the relativity of all forces, whether applied in the physical world as existent to-day, or that existence in man's earthly existence before, for the relativity of one force applies to another. Hence all relative forces apply to man's development, whether mental, physical or spiritual.

Reading 900-274

(Q) Will you give us, then, first, a definition of evolution, in a few words, such as Spencer gave in 1872, and such as [900] is struggling to give in this year?

(A) The conditions present themselves to the mind that views this as given, in this manner. Then, evolution, that form of the various conditions as combine themselves from the various forces as are manifest in the material plane into that ability of the combination of the various forms from one mass to another, in the various kingdoms of that force first given off by the first mind energy, or the All Creative Force, or the changing from the heterogeneous forces to that of the *elemental* forces, with its abilities to create within that as it propagates from one to another, see?

(Q) A certain kind or developed creative energy manifests in the heterogeneous integrated phase as matter, and another kind, of the same principle, manifests as animal.

(A) Correct, see? for just as the divisions as has been given, and as has been shown, how that when any energy that creates one force is brought together in that same force, the same force or energy is created, whether animal, whether vegetable, whether mineral, or what not. Each being a phase of that first Creative Energy, with man the highest representative of that Energy manifest in the material or earth plane.

(Q) Explain the development or evolutionary process in the first principle by which that kind of principle is concentrated to invert itself into matter, and another kind stored to become integrated into instinct, or animal, and lastly the same process manifesting another kind of creative activity, as man.

(A) This may only be done through the mind turning self to an introspective condition, and first *assuming* conditions exist, for the finite mind to gain this conception, see? for we have an energy—or, as has been given, we have a flesh of birds, of beast, of one energy, of one nature, one of another—each propagating, as has been set forth from the first—yet we come back to the first same principle: What created the first energy, or what IS the Creative Energy, or God? Then, we do not set that energy as a super man, more than the energy of heat, rather than that of animal or of tissue, or of any element, [is] able to create or propagate itself for each has *innate* within, from the first concept, that ability of creative forces, see?

(Q) Then, the intellect, as Bergsen says, must do a hand spring and transcend itself to find the essence of its own self.

(A) Must turn itself inside out, as it were, see? for it must become introspective, rather than outro [outer?] or extrospective [extroversive], see?

(Q) But this principle, in the first two degrees—matter and animal—is constantly repeating its integrating and disintegrating process. In man similarly, yet how does this process prove exceptional to that phase of man, or that entity of creative force that does *not* repeat this activity?

(A) For man [was] given that ability, with will, to become One with the Creative Energy, made a little higher than the other energies, yet combining all, see?

We are through for the present.

Reading 276-3

In the material world life is of the *universal* consciousness, as all development through that known or called evolution of life in a material plane, and is a portion of a body from conception to the transition in what is called death. That which enters, as the soul, is that that would use, or be the companion of, that life-physical through any given period of existence in an earth's appearance. As the variations come, these are brought by the activities of those who—through their *own* desire—attract or detract those that would manifest in a particular body. See?

(Q) Why is there a difference, and what happened in the interim?

(A) A physical being, or life, as given, is from inception, and is of an universal consciousness—see? When a physical being, or body, as this body, is brought into being by birth into the *physical* world, the *interim* between that is as of *that* period when the decision is being made by *that* soul that would occupy *that* individual body.

Reading 276-7

Hence, as indicated, how well may the body control those that are of a mental state in their evolution or development in material things! and thus partake more of materiality, yet motivative by the same spirit or life.

Again how well, how excellent, may the expressions of the purely mental body find those spiritual things that lead to the expression in the activities of the body as to bring into manifested form—either by the deeds done in the body, the activities of the physical self, or the expressions that may be made through the activities of other portions—or of the sensory forces of same in speech.

Hence how glorious may be those things to which the body may attain, either from those forces of the earth—that may be termed a career—or a success—or that appear as a gift, or a genius, or an individual that is endowed with super-normal powers in its activity in the earth.

Again how well balanced, how simple, yet how true, how patient! yet how earnest, how enthusiastic! yet how determined, how well may all these attributes—that are often so contradictory in the experience of many—become manifested things and experiences in the activities of this mental being that is found in this body!

Well, then, that those who would influence, or direct or make for influencing the life and the experience of this entity in this formative period, be earnest, sincere, sure, and well-balanced in that which they would present in this entity's experience—either as example or precept. For, *some* day—in this experience—will the activities of this body-mind, this soul-mind, give expression to that it has been governed, ruled or influenced by in forming that which is to be the work of the body, of the physical body, of the mental body, and upon which the soul-being will in this experience feed.

Then, if this be true—those things that have just been said, the natural question that arises in the minds or experiences of those that would study psychic forces—or any of the philosophies that have to do or deal with the principles motivating the influences or activities of individuals in this earth's plane in the present—would be:

What has karma to do with this body, then? What is the fate, or the destiny, of such a soul? Has it already been determined as to what it may do, or be, for the very best? or has it been so set that the activities and the influences, the environs and the hereditary forces, are to alter?

These indeed are worthy questions, in the light of that which has been given.

If there be any virtue or truth in those things given in the spiritual or Christian or Jehovah-God faith, His laws are immutable. What laws are immutable, if truth and God Himself is a growing thing—yet an ever changeable, and yet "ever the same, yesterday and today and forever"?

These things, these words, to many minds become contradictory, but they are in their inception *not* contradictory; for Truth, Life, Light, Immortality, are only words that give expression to or convey a concept of one and the same thing.

Hence, Destiny is: "As ye sow, so shall ye reap." And like begets like! And the first law of nature, which is the material manifestation of spiritual law in a physical world, is self-propagation—which means that it seeks self-preservation and the activity of the same law that brought the thought of man (or the spirit of man) into existence—companionship!

What, then, is karma? And what is destiny? What has the soul done, in the spiritual, the material, the cosmic world or consciousness, respecting the knowledge or awareness of the laws being effective in his experience—whether in the earth, in the air, in heaven or in hell? These are ever one; for well has it been said, "Though I take the wings of the morning and fly unto the utmost parts of the heavens, Thou art there! Though I make my bed in hell, Thou art there! Though I go to the utmost parts of the earth, Thou art there! Truth, Life, God! Then, that which is cosmic—or destiny, or karma—depends upon what the soul has done about that it has become aware of.

What, you say, has this to do with this soul, this entity, that—as we have given—is well balanced and attuned as to that it will do; by its own activating forces of its will, its desire—that arise from its experiences in the mental, the spiritual and the material world? Because it is thus making its destiny, its karma! For, HE will stand in the stead. For, by sin came death; by the shedding of blood came freedom—freedom from a consciousness, into a greater consciousness.

So, in His promises do we live and move and have our being. Be patient. But know much may be done.

Reading 294-11

. . . for speech is the highest vibration that is reached in the animal kingdom, and in that respect man in his evolution is above that of the other creatures in the creation.

Reading 5755-2

Thus in the answers we may find that, though there may be worlds, many universes, even much as to solar systems, greater than our own that we enjoy in the present, this earthly experience on this earth is a mere speck when considered even with our own solar system. Yet the soul of man, thy soul, encompasses *all* in this solar system or in others.

For, we are joint heirs with that universal force we call God—if we seek to do His biddings.

Reading 1602-5

Thus in the experience of souls through their evolution in the material things of the earth, there has been brought just that same effect in the material affairs of the souls active in expressing or manifesting at this particular period or sphere of development.

Much of just this comprehending is indicated in some of those records that are now becoming more and more a part of man's experience, or awareness; in that the cosmic or universal or spiritual laws are bringing same into that category or phase of experience where they become a part of individual experience.

This may be indicated from the records in the rocks; it may be indicated in the pyramids—man's attempts to leave a sign to those who, in the spiritual comprehension of material associations in spirit, would interpret that which had been, that which is, and that which was to be.

Hence it is seen that there are interpretations that become a matter of the consciousness of the individual so making same.

Or, to return to the first premise, it depends upon which line is taken by such an individual making such interpretation; whether a pessimistic or an optimistic, or a positive or a negative; or (by negative we mean) one that sees the world, as related to the earth and its position in the universe, being damned irrespective of what souls do about same—taking little or no account of the words, the promises, yea the activities of Him. *He* manifested in the earth that as would bring to the seeker an awareness of the constructive influence of same.

This may be indicated or seen in the record according to the Book—which is as a sign, a guide to those who seek to know His ways, His purposes to man.

These interpretations of the promises, the pledges taken and given in the lives and activities—or during the phases of a sojourn of an individual soul, must be taken into account.

And then these indicate as to what is to come to pass, even through these periods of the earth's journey through space; "catching up," as it were, with Time.

And then the soul realizes—in his search for his Maker—the patience that was, is and will be manifested in Him; He that is the way, the truth and the light.

Again the interpretation of the signs and the omens becomes an individual experience. And each soul—as this entity—then is given the privilege, the opportunity to *live* such an activity in its relationships to its fellow man; filling, fulfilling, and interpreting that which has been indicated, in such measures and such manners as to bring hope and not fear, peace and not hate, that which is *constructive* and *not* destructive, into the lives and minds and hearts of others.

Reading 2390–7

The entity then, now known as [2390] was that one first completed in that physical evolution, as to being the perfect body—as indicated through the activity of the parents in the Temples of Sacrifice and in the Temple Beautiful. Thus the entity then, Tar-Ello, was the first of the fair face who also had fair hair and blue eyes; this indicating to the Priest a completing of the purpose that had been the physical intent in those activities undertaken.

There were not the considerations that even among crows there are at times white ones, nor that among those of the dark skin, flat-haired, there are occasionally the pure white.

Not that this is other than as the environ, and thus may be considered by some as an excuse.

To the entity: *do not* attempt to justify self, ever. Rather let thy purpose, thy desire, thy hope, thy faith, ever be—in purpose—to the glory of the Father through the Son, manifested in the earth, who *never—nev-*

er—attempted to supplant; only applied the laws of God in the spiritual, in the mental, and thus in the material brought miracles, the increase, the activity that overcame the laws of gravity. These *ye* may do, as the children of God. For to each that lives with and in keeping with the purposes of all to the glory of the Father, He gives power for such to become the children of God, brothers then with that way and purpose.

In the experience then, it became as the natural consequence that the entity became the ideal of the Priest, the inspiration to give greater stress upon those activities in the Temple of Sacrifice.

Thus did the entity, early, become that close companion of the Priest; ministering oft with the Priest in the ritual, the activities that gradually became more and more the requirements of the Priest, as individuals chose to become the channels for those unfoldments.

Reading 2982-1

Before that the entity was in the Egyptian land, when there were those activities just prior to the passing of the Priest; when many changes had been wrought by the attempts of the Priest to placate—not exactly placate but to *hurry* the evolution of body and of expression through the activities in the Temple of Sacrifice.

Reading 2823-3

The entity was among those groups who had come with the King, and was not of the Natives; though in its developments the entity was known as a Native because of its close associations with some of those through that experience.

Then the entity's activities were those that it may, or must, learn again—or as it has already experienced, as then—that of patience.

Many of the individuals who were associated with the Priest in the various offices, however, were tempted or taught—as it were—by the misinterpretation of the law by the Priest himself. For there was the attempt to placate the law of evolution. While those activities brought within themselves conditions that greatly improved the situations, they left in the mental self the applying of spiritual law to attain material desires—without the mental concepts being in accord.

A good lesson here for everyone to learn who would know the way of the Lord! Be patient, be just, be kind, be longsuffering, show brotherly love—and then don't worry about what's going to happen! but be sure you do these! When you get to the place where you would worry (this is for the entity), stop and pray! For why worry, when you can pray? For God is not mocked, and He remembers thee in thy sincerity in thy purpose.

Reading 1223-6

In giving a biographical account of the entity in the Egyptian experience as Tek-Le-On, it would be well that there be given for the entity—and much for the study of others—a background of the period; that there might be a more perfect understanding of the activities in the material sense in the earth's plane, of being purified in the Temple of Sacrifice for the propagation of a new race; also that it might be understood as to what are the sources of attraction to individuals with whom there may have been a connection in the material plane from experiences in the spiritual—or the application of an individual entity to spiritual laws through an earthly existence in associations with others.

That entity, Tek-Le-On, was among the offspring of those who were entangled in matter, yet with a spiritual import; yet having blemishes in the body that kept them—as individuals—from their associations with those of the race represented by the Priest in that experience.

Thus we find the entity was a daughter of those who were the children of that group so enmeshed. In the early experience, when the body was first presented by the mother to the Priest, the entity was among the first of the individuals to be offered in the Temple, called the Temple of Sacrifice, as ones who might be dedicated to the activities according to the theory or idea of the Priest as to how individuals might be prepared for the incoming of a different type, or a more perfect stature of man.

As there were then those activities which brought about this change, these brought hardships for the entity through its early experience; not only in its separation from its people but in its being regulated by ideas of an individual who had only ideas—though these in the light of the results might even in the present day be considered near to ideal, from a scientific point of view; yet from the purely mental and spiritual view might be called barbarous by some in the present.

Because, the limbs of this entity formed those activities that were part beast of the field, as would be called in the present. This not only to the Priest but to those helpers at the time offered the first problems, as to how—through mechanical as well as natural law as to cause and effect—there might not be reproduced such blemishes in the offspring of the body.

Thus in the experience for the first time there was found the eradication of that indicated in the flesh of the animal, in the lower or hind limbs or legs, that does not exist in the human being. While the expression is different in different animals, the projection through spirit projecting in matter, through the periods of the evolution, had *not* brought about the change of this gland—that is still existent in the animal in the material kingdom.

This was removed from the body—this body—by the operators, with the Priest, in that early stage of that group's interpretation of nature, as related to God's creation of man as a representative of the Godhead, and as to what those of the kind had brought into existence.

These activities brought periods of disturbance, as these glands were removed and then the body was subjected to those relationships which would bring the determining factor as to whether or not there had been the selecting or the correcting of that which had been determined as the source of such variations.

Then these brought about those connections, associations and relations, that were to the entity abhorrent; until there *was* the reproduction that was perfect in body, as well as those that had not been intermingled with those of that phase of man's physical evolution.

Reading 2079-1

For, indeed each entity, each soul, is in the process of evolution towards the First Cause. Much becomes evolution,—much may become involution.

From these aspects mentioned, we find that the entity becomes the student—one with the ability to give expression, to make pronouncements; and all too often there is the inclination, in the entity's application—as will be seen, to feel or to give expression in such a manner as to carry the impression into the consciousness of others that the self is the last word—in whatever activity the entity may be engaged, or in whatever purpose that may be chosen by the entity for giving its expression.

3

●

Creation and Evolution

Reading 3976-8

In the beginning when chaos existed in the creating of the earth, the Spirit of God moved over the face of same and out of chaos came the world—with its beauty in natural form, or in nature.

With man's advent into the world, then personalities, individualities, began to find expressions in *subduing* the earth, and man—with his natural bent—not only attempted to subdue the *earth*, but to subdue one another; and the result was the differences of opinions, the various sects, sets, classes and races.

As the earth was peopled, and the abilities of expansion were able to bring the various groups, or associations of groups or nations, they *could*—and *did*—withdraw into themselves, and build for themselves in the various portions of the world that known as the periods of advancement of some particular group of peoples.

As the world has advanced, all the various phases of man's developments have entered to make a different phase, either in the political, economic, or religious aspect of man's experience. In the various portions, then, of the world there has been builded those necessary developments for that particular group or portion of those peoples, or those developments of those peoples in their particular line.

With the advent of the closeness of the worlds coming into being, so that the man upon the other side of the world is as much the neighbor as the man next door, more and more have been the turmoils that have arisen in the attempt of individual leaders or groups to induce, force or compel, one portion of the world to think as the other, or the other group to dwell together as brethren with one bond of sympathy, or one standard for all.

With the present conditions, then, that exist—these have all come to that place in the development of the human family where there must be a reckoning, a one point upon which all may agree, that out of all of this turmoil that has arisen from the social life, racial differences, the outlook upon the relationship of man to the Creative Forces or his God, and his relationships one with another, must come to some *common* basis upon which all *may* agree. You say at once, such a thing is impractical, impossible! What has caused the present conditions, not alone at home but abroad? It is that realization that was asked some thousands of years ago, "Where *is* thy brother? His blood *cries* to me from the ground!" and the other portion of the world has answered, *is* answering, "Am I my brother's keeper?" The world, *as* a world—that makes for the disruption, for the discontent—has lost its ideal. Man may not have the same *idea*. Man—*all* men—may have the same *ideal*!

As the Spirit of God once moved to bring peace and harmony out of chaos, so must the Spirit move over the earth and magnify itself in the hearts, minds and souls of men to bring peace, harmony and understanding, that they may dwell together in a way that will bring that peace, that harmony, that can only come with all having the one Ideal; not the one idea, but "Thou shalt love the Lord Thy God with all thine heart, thy neighbor *as* thyself!" This [is] the whole law, this [is] the whole answer to the world, to each and every soul. That is the answer to the world conditions as they exist today.

Text of Reading 5749-14 [Entire reading]

HLC: You will have before you the enquiring mind of the entity, Thomas Sugrue, present in this room, and certain of the problems which confront him in composing the manuscript of *There Is a River*. The entity is now ready to describe the philosophical concepts which have been given through this source, and wishes to parallel and align them with known religious tenets, especially those of Christian theology. The entity does not wish to set forth a system of thought, nor imply that all questions of a philosophical nature can be answered through this source—the limitations of the finite mind prevent this. But the entity wishes to answer those questions which will naturally arise in the mind of the reader, and many of the questions which are being asked by all people in the world today. Therefore the entity presents certain problems and questions, which you will answer as befits the entity's understanding and the task of interpretation before him.

EC: Yes, we have the enquiring mind, Thomas Sugrue, and those problems, those questions that arise in the mind of the entity at this period. Ready for questions.

(Q) The first problem concerns the reason for creation. Should this be given as God's desire to experience Himself, God's desire for companionship, God's desire for expression, or in some other way?

(A) God's desire for companionship and expression.

(Q) The second problem concerns that which is variously called evil, darkness, negation, sin. Should it be said that this condition existed as a necessary element of creation, and the soul, given free will, found itself with the power to indulge in it, or lose itself in it? Or should it be said that this is a condition created by the activity of the soul itself? Should it be described, in either case, as a state of consciousness, a gradual lack of awareness of self and self's relation to God?

(A) It is the free will and its losing itself in its relationship to God.

(Q) The third problem has to do with the fall of man. Should this be described as something which was inevitable in the destiny of souls, or something which God did not desire, but which He did not prevent once He had given free will? The problem here is to reconcile the omniscience of God and His knowledge of all things with the free will of the soul and the soul's fall from grace.

(A) He did not prevent, once having given free will. For, He made the individual entities or souls in the beginning. For, the beginnings of sin, of course, were in seeking expression of themselves outside of the plan or the way in which God had expressed same. Thus it was the individual, see? Having given free will, then—though having the foreknowledge, though being omnipotent and omnipresent—it is only when the soul that is a portion of God *chooses* that God knows the end thereof.

(Q) The fourth problem concerns man's tenancy on earth. Was it originally intended that souls remain out of earthly forms, and were the races originated as a necessity resulting from error?

(A) The earth and its manifestations were only the expression of God and not necessarily as a place of tenancy for the souls of men, until man was created—to meet the needs of existing conditions.

(Q) The fifth problem concerns an explanation of the Life Readings. From a study of these it seems that there is a trend downward, from early incarnations, toward greater earthliness and less mentality. Then there is a swing upward, accompanied by suffering, patience, and understanding. Is this the normal pattern, which results in virtue and oneness with God obtained by free will and mind?

(A) This is correct. It is the pattern as it is set in Him.

(Q) The sixth problem concerns interplanetary and inter-system dwelling, between earthly lives. It was given through this source that the entity Edgar Cayce, after the experience as Uhjltd [in an ancient Persian incarnation], went to the system of Arcturus, and then returned to earth. Does this indicate a usual or an unusual step in soul evolution?

(A) As indicated, or as has been indicated in other sources besides this as respecting this very problem—Arcturus is that which may be called the center of this universe, through which individuals pass and at which period there comes the choice of the individual as to whether it is to return to complete there—that is, in this planetary system, our sun, the earth sun and its planetary system—or to pass on to others. This was an unusual step, and yet a usual one.

(Q) The seventh problem concerns implications from the sixth problem. Is it necessary to finish the solar system cycle before going to other systems?

(A) Necessary to finish the solar cycle.

(Q) Can oneness be attained—or the finish of evolution reached—on any system, or must it be in a particular one?

(A) Depending upon what system the entity has entered, to be sure. It may be completed in any of the many systems.

(Q) Must the solar cycle be finished on earth, or can it be completed on another planet, or does each planet have a cycle of its own which must be finished?

(A) If it is begun on the earth it must be finished on the earth. The solar system of which the earth is a part is only a portion of the whole. For, as indicated in the number of planets about the earth, they are of one and the same—and they are relative one to another. It is the cycle of the whole system that is finished, see?

(Q) The eighth problem concerns the pattern made by parents at conception. Should it be said that this pattern attracts a certain soul because it approximates conditions which that soul wishes to work with?

(A) It approximates conditions. It does not set. For, the individual entity or soul, given the opportunity, has its own free will to work in or out of those problems as presented by that very union. Yet the very union, of course, attracts or brings a channel or an opportunity for the expression of an individual entity.

(Q) Does the incoming soul take on of necessity some of the parents' karma? (A) Because of its relative relationship to same, yes. Otherwise, no.

(Q) Does the soul itself have an earthly pattern which fits back into the one created by the parents?

(A) Just as indicated, it is relative—as one related to another; and because of the union of activities they are brought in the pattern. For in such there is the explanation of universal or divine laws, which are ever one and the same; as indicated in the expression that God moved within Himself and then He didn't change, though did bring to Himself that of His own being made crucified even in the flesh.

(Q) Are there several patterns which a soul might take on, depending on what phase of development it wished to work upon—i.e., could a soul choose to be one of several personalities, any of which would fit its individuality?

(A) Correct.

(Q) Is the average fulfillment of the soul's expectation more or less than fifty percent?

(A) It's a continuous advancement, so it is more than fifty percent.

(Q) Are hereditary, environment and will equal factors in aiding or retarding the entity's development?

(A) Will is the greater factor, for it may overcome any or all of the others; provided that will is made one with the pattern, see? For, no influence of heredity, environment or what not, surpasses the will; else why would there have been that pattern shown in which the individual soul, no matter how far astray it may have gone, may enter with Him into the holy of holies?

(Q) The ninth problem concerns the proper symbols, or similes, for the Master, the Christ. Should Jesus be described as the soul who first went through the cycle of earthly lives to attain perfection, including perfection in the planetary lives also?

(A) He should be. This is as the man, see?

(Q) Should this be described as a voluntary mission One Who was already perfected and returned to God, having accomplished His Oneness in other planes and systems?

(A) Correct.

(Q) Should the Christ-Consciousness be described as the awareness within each soul, imprinted in pattern on the mind and waiting to be awakened by the will, of the soul's oneness with God?

(A) Correct. That's the idea exactly!

(Q) Please list the names of the incarnations of the Christ, and of Jesus, indicating where the development of the man Jesus began.

(A) First, in the beginning, of course; and then as Enoch, Melchizedek, in the perfection. Then in the earth of Joseph, Joshua, Jeshua, Jesus.

(Q) The tenth problem concerns the factors of soul evolution. Should mind, the builder, be described as the last development because it should not unfold until it has a firm foundation of emotional virtues?

(A) This might be answered Yes and No, both. But if it is presented in that there is kept, willfully, see, that desire to be in the at-onement, then it is necessary for that attainment before it recognizes mind as the way.

(Q) The eleventh problem concerns a parallel with Christianity. Is Gnosticism the closest type of Christianity to that which is given through this source?

(A) This is a parallel, and was the commonly accepted one until there began to be set rules in which there were the attempts to take short cuts. And there are none in Christianity!

(Q) What action of the early church, or council, can be mentioned as that which ruled reincarnation from Christian theology?

(A) Just as indicated—the attempts of individuals to accept or take advantage of, because of this knowledge, see?

(Q) Do souls become entangled in other systems as they did in this system?

(A) In other systems that represent the same as the earth does in this system, yes.

(Q) Is there any other advice which may be given to this entity at this time in the preparation of these chapters?

(A) Hold fast to that ideal, and using Him ever as the Ideal. And hold up that *necessity* for each to meet the same problems. And *do not* attempt to shed or to surpass or go around the Cross. *This* is that upon which each and every soul *must* look and know it is to be borne in self *with* Him.

We are through for the present.

Reading 262–123

(Q) How does Spirit compare with mind?

(A) Spirit is the First Cause. Mind is an effect, or an active force that partakes of spiritual as well as material import. Mind is an essence or a flow between Spirit and that which is made manifest materially.

(Q) Just how should we explain the division of Spirit (into what we know as Good and Evil) in the spiritual realm before the earth was created?

(A) God, the First Cause, in spirit, created in spirit the separate influences or forces that are a portion of, and manifested in the spirit of, God. In that essence, to become materially manifested through the evolution of the spirit of God, sin first began.

(Q) Are we correct in assuming that the first spiritual beings created were made up of Mind, Spirit and Will?

(A) The first concept as may be had of that in materiality is that it is an essence, without form, save as it begins to manifest—as would be gas, odor, wind, smoke—yet that it has with it the will, the mind, the power to make manifest by that with which, in which, it manifests, as does also odor, gas, wind and the like. Thus—as the activities came—we may assume that the First Cause was Spirit, Mind, Will.

(Q) How much of an explanation should we give of Adam and Eve as God's projection and how should we handle this?

(A) As has been indicated, this should be the interpretation of each member of the group, as they as individuals have reacted or do react to same. As to the presentation of same here, do not make same obnoxious but state it in such a manner that there is little or no ground for refutation of same.

(Q) Are time and space concepts that exist outside of physical consciousness?

(A) No. For the physical consciousness is an activity that uses such, as the divisions of space and time. And in patience only may ye become aware of the concept of either.

Reading 3744–5

(Q) What are the laws governing relativity of all force?

(A) In giving the manifestation of such an law, which does exist, we first must consider that, that is called force, and that force then in its relation, or the relativity of that force to all force.

There are, as were set in the beginning, as far as the concern is of this physical earth plane, those rules or laws in the relative force of those that govern the earth, and the beings of the earth plane, and also that same law governs the planets, stars, constellations, groups, that that constitutes the sphere, the space, in which the planet moves. These are of the one force, and we see the manifestation of the relation of one force with another in the many various phases as is shown, for in fact that which to the human mind exists, in fact does not exist, for it has been in past before it is to the human mind in existence.

In this, we see the law of the relations of conditions, space or time and its relation to human mind, as is capable of obtaining information upon the earth plane from a normal force or conditions. Hence, we bring the same word, relativity of force, to prove its own self, and condition, for we have as in this:

The earth in its motion, held in space by that force of attraction, or detraction, or gravitation, or lack of gravitation in its force, so those things that do appear to have reality, and their reality to the human mind, have in reality passed into past conditions before they have reached the mind, for with the earth's laws, and its relations to other spheres, has to man become a past condition. So it is reached only in the further forces as will show, and as is given, for man to understand in this developing, or this evolution from sphere to sphere, or from plane to plane, in this condition.

Hence, we find to the normal mind, there is no law as to relativity of force, save as the individual may apply same in the individual's needs of them. That is sufficient…

(Q) Give the best method of helping the human family increase in knowledge of the subconscious soul or spirit world.

(A) The knowledge of the subconscious of an entity, or an individual, in or of the human family, is as of one integral force, or element, or self in the creation of the human family, and until the entity, or individual, as individuals, make this known to groups, classes, countries, nations, *the greater study of self*, that force will only be magnified. That of the spirit is the spark, or portion of the Divine that is in every entity, whether complete or of the evolution to that completeness.

The study from the human standpoint, of subconscious, subliminal, psychic, soul forces, is and should be the great study for the human family, for through self man will understand its Maker when it understands its relation to its Maker, and it will only understand that through itself, and that understanding is the knowledge as is given here in this state.

Each and every person getting that understanding has its individual force toward the great creation, and its individual niche, place or unit to perform. Has to reach numbers of psychic forces or phenomena that may be manifested in the earth plane, all the same, yet the understanding for the individual entity, viewed from its own standpoint, with its knowledge, is obtained and made ready by itself, to be manifested through itself, towards its own development, and in that development of the creation or world. In this manner, and in this form, and in this way, will the development (*to study the force as given through this manner*) be of assistance to the world.

As in dreams, those forces of the subconscious, when taken or correlated into those forms that relate to the various phases of the individual, give to that individual the better understanding of self, when correctly interpreted, or when correctly answered.

Forget not that it has been said correctly that the Creator, the Gods and the God of the Universe, speak to man through this individual self. Man approaches the nearer condition of its approach to that field when the normal is at rest; sleep or slumber, and when more of the forces are taken into consideration, and are studied by the individual (not someone else) it is the individual's job, each individual's condition, each individual's position, each individual's relation, each individual's manifestation, each individual's receiving the message from the higher forces themselves, and for each individual to understand if they will study, to show themselves approved.

"In all thy getting, my son, get understanding." [Prov. 4:7] That of Self.

When one understands self, and self's relation to its Maker, the duty to
its neighbor, its own duty to self, it cannot, it will not be false to man,
or to its Maker. Give then more thought, *for thoughts are deeds*, and are
children of the relation reached between the mental and the soul, and
has its relation to spirit and soul's plane of existence, as they do in the
physical or earth plane. What one thinks continually, they become;
what one cherishes in their heart and mind they make a part of the
pulsation of their heart, through their own blood cells, and build in
their own physical, that which its spirit and soul must feed upon, and
that with which it will be possessed, when it passes into the realm for
which the other experiences of what it has gained here in the physical
plane, must be used.

The attributes of the soul and spirit are as many, and as many more,
as the attributes of the physical or mental mind. Each, in the beginning,
endowed with that same condition—position. Each, in itself, building
to itself, through its development known through the ages, as called
from the earth plane, that which is manifest upon the earth. With
each development, that force, known upon the plane as *will*, is given
to man over and above all creation; *that* force that may separate itself
from its Maker, for with the *will* man may either adhere or contradict
the Divine law—those immutable laws, as are set between the Creator
and the created.

The study of these, through their phases and forms, and especially
through any of those phases, wherein the carnal or material or normal
forces are laid aside, and the ever present elements of spirit and soul
commune with those of the forces as found in each entity. Study those
and *know thyself.*

Reading 900-340

(Q) Now let's see—in environment and heredity—

(A) Much has been given as regarding these various conditions as
have been presented to the body, for in acquiring the perfect understanding of hereditary conditions and environnmental conditions, let
not hereditary mean only that of the present generation, see? That is the
entity. We have begun to reason from inside out. Not from outside in.

Though the illustrations may be presented that are seen from outside in.

In environmental conditions, a great study has been made recently by Brennan concerning this very condition, in which there are some twenty thousand of the illiterates and the ones who have been termed as weak minded that have lived in an environmental condition until the condition itself has presented that as from the scientific standpoint of being the cause of insanity.

Then, in the presentation of hereditary conditions, and of environmental conditions, we find by the comparison of these two, this presents quite a condition to be reckoned with, and—as has been for the ages past, and will be for ages onward—the study of man as to whether environmental or heredity [conditions] produce the greater part in the one development. The answer is the application ever of will in either condition. Reckoning then as to whether will has been applied in more of the earth experiences, or has that of environmental used, rather than been used by the entity itself. Get the point? *has* the entity in its experience through its will *applied* that of will toward the development, or has it allowed itself to be used by the environment and become subject to environment, or has it developed itself through its will towards its own hereditary position—for *all* are the children of God. How has the development led?

(Q) Now, let's take the animal. One great belief at the present time is the survival of the fittest—

(A) Applies in the *animal* kingdom—not in man!

(Q) That's a touchy point, and it will take a lot of explanation on my part.

(A) Let all read history! Which has survived—the brute strength, or the development towards that of God? Which survives—the man that studies God and seeks to emulate His forces and powers, or the man that emulates the forces of earth or flesh? This answers itself!

(Q) Well, now I take it that misapplication of creation, or of the coming into being of environment is correct—that is, the pushing of its way finally into liquid state and then carrying on into the mineral kingdom, vegetable kingdom, and lower animals of this original homogeneity, and then the coordination of its elements to push further into a two dimensional environmental condition that—carrying on in a duplication process—builds up in the lower kingdoms that called heredity.

(A) Correct. Yet we find this may be carried to that very same extent, unless there is taken into consideration that as this condition existed, as this evolution began in the mind of the Creator, there then came the point, the place, the beginning, when that as created was *given* that as was necessary to make its development by applying these same forces *one* with that Creative Energy. Hence the next creation.

(Q) I have to study this.

(A) That is, the kingdoms then being termed in the manner in which the conception may be gained better of this in earth's plane we are dealing with, alone, in this kingdom we find first, as the worlds created—and are still in creation in this heterogeneous mass as is called the outer sphere, or those portions as man looks up to in space, the mists that are gathering—what's the beginning of this? In this same beginning, so began the earth's sphere. The earth's sphere, with the first creation in the mind of the Creator, has kept its same Creative Energy, for God is the same yesterday, today and forever, and same in one creation creates that same in the other creation. One keeps right on through with the other, see? Now, as this mass has pushed up into that wherein it reverses itself, as it were, making then its own environmental condition, and the survival of the stronger of these came to that as the animal kingdom, see? Now, as this came into the animal kingdom, then correct is that as is said, "God said, we will make man." Then man, the creation in itself, that combining all of the forms of creation so far created, that that same force might understand by having passed through that same creation as was necessary to bring up to that dividing point between man and animal and plant, and mineral kingdom—*given* then the will, and the soul, that it might make itself One with that Creation. Now, that will, then, is heredity. That environment is the evolution. There you have reincarnation, there you have evolution, there you have the mineral kingdom, the plant kingdom, the animal kingdom, each developing towards its own source, yet all belonging and becoming one in that force as it develops itself to become one with the Creative Energy, and one with the God. The one then surviving in the earth, through mineral, through plant kingdom, through the vegetable kingdom, through the animal kingdom, each as the geological survey shows, held its sway in the earth, pass from one into the other; yet man given that to be lord over all, and the *only* survivor of that creation.

Reading 2067–1

Men's (and women's) activities are to sow the seed. It's God's part, and promise, to give the increase. It is an answering again of spirit to spirit, the quickening, the enlivening, the life-giving. For, God and love alone are life in its essence.

All else are but lines to those forces, for God in His love and in His wisdom has sought such as companions with Him in the movement which began from "God moved and there was light."

In thy movements, then, let thy thoughts, thy purposes, thy hopes, thy desires, ever be towards that of light. Not as light of the sun, or even of the stars—for these are but reflections of that *glorious* light which is in the *son* of God, who is thy light, thy Brother—yea, thy Lord, thy God!

Reading 1602–3

(Q) Three hundred years ago Jacob Boehme decreed Atlantis would rise again at this crisis time when we cross from this Piscean Era into the Aquarian. Is Atlantis rising now? Will it cause a sudden convolution and about what Year?

(A) In 1998 we may find a great deal of the activities as have been wrought by the gradual changes that are coming about. These are at the periods when the cycle of the solar activity, or the years as related to the sun's passage through the various spheres of activity become paramount or Catamount [?] [Tantamount?] to the change between the Piscean and the Aquarian age. This is a gradual, not a cataclysmic activity in the experience of the earth in this period.

(Q) The "Primitive Man in Light" looked out from the earth and saw us within the sphere of the Universe with its constellations which combined to form his consciousness. He knew then, that a "Way of Escape" from the rounds of Reincarnation opened beyond this Universe—beyond the Galaxy—beyond the opening in the forehead of Cepheus. Will you explain this "Way of Escape"?

(A) We do not find it so. For we have this: These are the basis of—Let's get what is the first principle here. These are concepts, these are not the activities of individuals who look out upon that; not as the earth as the center of its activities, but as the own solar system, here. It is true that the activities so far as in this sphere or Galaxy of activities of the planetary forces within this present solar system, the earth first became as the indwelling of the consciousness of the race or the man in this particular sphere, but sin—the separation—that as caused the separation of souls from the universal consciousness—came not in the sphere of materiality first, but in that of spirit. For what *is* that as just indicated that makes for the choice, or produces the saying by the teachers or sages that "no one may come except he be called of God"? That is, that the activities of the individuals through the various actions or consciousness or awareness in the various spheres of activity *become as* a part of the divine plan for the return, only *through* the reincarnation into the actions in which choices may be made by the individual for the alleviating or the satisfying or for the development of the individual entity or soul to be in the awareness of being itself and in relationship to the Creative Forces as become one with Him—even as has been shown by the necessity of the first begotten, the only begotten of the Father to enter into the material plane as the first consciousness or awareness of its being able in itself to choose for its activity independent of materiality where those activities became, and become, manifest as a part of the whole consciousness. Hence the awareness of the soul as to its separateness, or its being separated, only comes through the manifestations of the principles of that cosmic consciousness in materiality. Hence it is as evolution in a part of the development of the whole of the universe; not this consciousness of our own solar system, but of that about all solar force, or which our own system is only a mere part of the whole consciousness. But in the earth and man's awareness into the three-dimensional consciousness, only those that have entered same may relieve or leave same through the awareness of there being those influences through their various spheres of activity, including not only the earthly sojourns or material sojourns as we know in a physical consciousness, but the sojourns throughout the spheres of activity when they are absent from a physical or material consciousness ...

(Q) What will the Aquarian Age mean to mankind as regards Physical, Mental and Spiritual development? Is the Aquarian Age described as the "Age of the Lily" and why?

(A) Think Ye this might be answered in a word? These are as growths. What meant that awareness as just indicated? In the Piscean age, in the center of same, we had the entrance of Emmanuel or God among men, see? What did that mean? The same will be meant by the full consciousness of the ability to communicate with or to be aware of the relationships to the Creative Forces and the uses of same in material environs. This awareness during the era or age in the age of Atlantis and Lemuria or Mu brought what?

Destruction to man, and his beginning of the needs of the journey up through that of selfishness. Then, as to what will these be—*only* those who accept same will even become aware of what's going on about them! How few realize the vibratory forces as create influences from even one individual to another, when they are even in the same vibratory force or influence! And yet ye ask what will the Aquarian age bring in mind, in body, in experience?

(Q) Is the Aquarian Age described as the 'Age of the Lily' and why?

(A) The purity. Only the purity as it represents will be able to comprehend or understand that awareness that is before those who seek the way.

Reading 900–10

(Q) As created by God in the first, are souls perfect, and if so, why any need of development?

(A) In this we find only the answer in this: The evolution of life as may be understood by the finite mind. In the first cause, or principle, all is perfect. In the creation of soul, we find the portion may become a living soul and equal with the Creator. To reach that position, when separated, must pass through all stages of development, that it may be one with the Creator. As we have is this: Man. In the beginning, we find the spirit existent in all living force. When such force becomes inanimate in finite forces [it is] called dead; not necessarily losing its usefulness, either to Creator, or created, in material world. In that of creation of man, we find all the elements in a living, moving, world, or an element in itself; yet without that experience as of a first cause, yet endowed with all the various modifications of elements or forces manifested in each. For first there is the spirit, then soul (man we are speaking of), then mind with its various modifications and with its various incentives, with its various ramifications, if you please, and the will the balance in the force that may make all or lose all. In the developing, then, that the man may be one with the Father, necessary that the soul pass, with its companion the will, through all the various stages of development, until the will is lost in Him and he becomes one with the Father. In the illustration of this, we find in the man as called Jesus. In this: This man, as man, makes the will the will of the Father, then becoming one with the Father and the model for man.

(Q) Does the soul choose the planet to which it goes after each incarnation? If not, what force does?

(A) In the Creation, we find all force relative one with the other, and in the earth's plane that of the flesh. In the developing from plane to plane becomes the ramification, or the condition of the will merited in its existence finding itself through eons of time. In the illustration, or manifestation in this, we find again in the man called Jesus. When the soul reached that development in which it reached earth's plane, it became in the flesh the model, as it had reached through the developments in those spheres, or planets, known in earth's plane, obtaining then One in All. As in Mercury pertaining of Mind. In Mars of Madness. In Earth as of Flesh. In Venus as Love. In Jupiter as Strength. In Saturn as the beginning of earthly woes, that to which all insufficient matter is cast for the beginning. In that of Uranus as of the Psychic. In that of Neptune as of Mystic. In Septimus as of Consciousness. In Arcturus as of the developing. As to various constellations, and of groups, only these ramifications of the various existences experienced in the various conditions.

(Q) What is meant by the Borderland as referred to in a reading?

(A) That condition that the living experience with the soul, the mental faculties, the desire, the consciousness of the various phases of each laid aside and the soul, with its companion, the sub-conscious, peeps into the interlay between the spirit and soul, or superconscious, or that existence as lies in that space where the impressions of the disincarnate spirits, with their soul, communicate with such earthly conditions as illustrated in this: When the physical body lies in slumber, we find the organs that are subjugated, the life-giving flow and the subconscious forces acting, and the soul forces ready for that communication with intermingling conditions lying between. Again, as in the present sphere, in this body lying here [EC], we find all life in suspension, only portions of the higher vibrations in accord with those vibrations that communicate with the Universal forces.

(Q) What is meant by destiny?

(A) In the Creation, we find each given condition has its condition and it attributes, with its law. The end of any law [is] destiny, which may be variegated, changed, by the various modifications, with the meeting of other laws, which does not change the destiny of a law or force. Just as is illustrated in a common condition: A stick placed in water appears bent. In fact it is straight.

Reading 900-422

(Q) Does that represent a different kind of vibration?

(A) All force is vibration, as all comes from one central vibration and its activity into, out from, and its own creative forces, as given, with that of the divine as manifested in man, is same vibration—taking different form. Here, we may give a dissertation, in a manner, as to what Creative Energy is, as related to man and his activity, and as the forces as are seen and about man. As has been given, true it was said, "Come let us make man in our image," in his own image created God, or created by God, was man. Then containing all of the vibrations that were without, were given into that whole being of man—which in *its* vibration gave man the soul. *above* all else created, see? Then we see how the evolution of force in vibration brought up to the point wherein man becomes one *with* the Creative Energy, or the Godhead—*with* the ability to become that that he is *not* at the beginning, by making himself absent from the will of the Creator or Creative Energy. How? In that the ability to create mentally, and with the hand *makes* that which *is* the created force of that mind, and with that may make destructive forces for self. Hence man becomes one *with* the Creative Energy, or away *from* that Creative Energy. When man makes himself one *with*—then all things were created by him, without him there was nothing created that was created, or made—and are then *his* by rightful heir, even as shown in His Son, wherein man [is] shown the way, or the access to this all Creative Energy.

Reading 262-99

EC: Yes, we have the group as gathered here, as a group, as individuals and their work on the lesson Knowledge.

That which has been given and as gathered here is very good, needing those correlations of ideals, experiences, purpose, intent, and then the application of same in the experience of those that would make Knowledge as a part of themselves, in their search, in their way, in their application of that as may be manifested in their experience *in* the application of that as has been given.

For this, as you each will find, do find, should be in your experience a real turning point in your *individual*, personal experience; as you each have emptied yourselves, as you each have laid the ground work as it were of that indeed as was given to man, *"subdue* the earth." For all therein has been given for man's purpose, for man's convenience, for man's understanding, for man's interpreting of God's relationship to man. And when man makes same only a gratifying, a satisfying of self, whether in appetite, in desire, in selfish motives for self–aggrandizement, self–exaltation, these become—as from old—stumblingblocks. But he that hath put off the old and put on the new is regenerated in the new Adam, in the last Adam, in the Christ. And as many as have done so may find in themselves that Knowledge of His presence abiding with them; so that things, conditions, circumstances, environs, no longer become stumblingblocks—rather have they become stepping–stones for the greater view wherein they each may gain at least in part first, gradually growing in grace, in the understanding to know those glories, those beauties God hath prepared for them that know the way of the Cross *with* the Christ as the good shepherd. For He will call each by name, for He knoweth His sheep and He is the good shepherd to those that put their trust, their lives, their troubles, their joys, their sorrows, their understandings, in Him. For He hath taken the burden of the world. Will ye then join with Him in this acceptable year of the Lord and know that to do good is Knowledge . . . ?

(Q) Please explain the following from rdg. [262–96, Par. 11] May 24, 1936: "For the soul had understanding before he partook of the flesh in which the choice was to be made." Why (if the soul had understanding) the necessity to take flesh in order to make the choice?

(A) Considereth thou that Spirit hath its manifestations, or does it *use* manifestations for its activity? The Spirit of God is aware through activity, and we see it in those things celestial, terrestrial, of the air, of all forms. And *all* of these are merely manifestations! The Knowledge, the understanding, the comprehending, then necessitated the entering in because it partook of that which *was* in manifestation; and thus the *perfect* body, the celestial body, became an earthly body and thus put on flesh. (The explanation to some becomes worse than the first! This, then:) (This has nothing to do with Knowledge, or it is too much knowledge for some of you, for you'll stumble over it; but you asked for it and here it is!) When the earth became a dwelling place for matter, when gases formed into those things that man sees in nature and in activity about him, then matter began its ascent in the various forms of physical evolution—in the *mind* of God! The spirit chose to enter (celestial, not an earth spirit—he hadn't come into the earth yet!), chose to put on, to become a part of that which was as a command not to be done! Then those so entering *must* continue through the earth until the body–mind is made perfect for the soul, or the body–celestial again.

Reading 1610–2

EC: Yes, we have the records here of that entity now known as or called [1610]—the records upon time and space.

And these are a portion of the entity's application through the sojourns in the astrological environs as well as the material sojourns in the earth; the records being made upon time and space according to the application of self through will, as to that held by the entity through its experience.

Hence it is both evolution *and* growth. (Consider the difference!)

In giving the interpretations, these portions of same are chosen with the desire and the hope that they may be made a helpful experience for the entity; in a way and manner that the applying of self as is understood from the shortcomings or from the virtues and vices in the varied experiences may enable the entity to take hope—that there may be a fulfilling of the purpose for which self enters each and every experience.

For each soul through the material or three-dimensional plane has the opportunity to manifest all phases of virtue or vice. The whole sin, ever, is selfishness—or its children.

Hence, as there is given the good or the bad, there is the desire that there may be such a choice within the experience of the entity as to know whereunto it has been called. For to manifest through associations with others that which is the Law of One, the experiences that may glorify and magnify the consciousness of the Divine—these are the purposes, these are the ways and manners.

For each soul has and does become aware of its separation from the

Father, God. It seeks not justification in itself but through the promises in Him to again come into that presence, that consciousness, that one-ness in such a manner as to know itself to be itself, yet one with that Creative Force or God—even as He ...

The activities, of course, will be in individual natures or influenc-es, yet it is the relationship as one bears to another in such activities; whether in the direction in which there may be the training of individ-uals for definite or special service or activity, or in such relationships to keep the body more physically fit. All portions of same are taken into consideration, rather than the one—or the developing of one, save where a lack of coordination has been brought about by an *inconsider-ation* of this unity of body, mind, soul.

As these are one manifested in a physical body, so must the body view the physical, the mental, the spiritual activities of his own rela-tionships to others as well as the relationships to the whole.

For each entity, each activity is dependent one upon another. In some of those relationships or sports or games ye may term this perfect timing. Time in that sense is not relative to even the whole as a spiritual entity but as the relationships of physical activity to the mental purpose for which the physical activity is called into being.

Reading 3744–4

(Q) Do the planets have an effect on the life of every individual born?

(A) They have. Just as this earth's forces were set in motion, and about it, those forces that govern the elements, elementary so, of the earth's sphere or plane, and as each comes under the influence of those conditions, the influence is to the individual without regards to the will, which is the developing factor of man, in which such is expressed through the breath of the Creator, and as one's plane of existence is lived out from one sphere to another they come under the influence of those to which it passes from time to time. In the sphere of many of the planets within the same solar system, we find they are banished to certain conditions in developing about the spheres from which they pass, and again and again and again return from one to another until they are prepared to meet the everlasting Creator of our entire Uni-verse, of which our system is only a very small part. Be not dismayed [deceived]; God is not mocked; "Whatsoever a man soweth that shall he also reap." [Gal. 6:7] In the various spheres, then, through which he must pass to attain that which will fit him for the conditions to enter in, and become a part of that Creator, just as an individual is a part of the creation now. In this manner we see there is the influence of the planets upon an individual, for all must come under that influence, though one may pass from one plane to another without going through all stages of the condition, for only upon the earth plane at present do we find man is flesh and blood, but upon others do we find those of his own making in the preparation of his own development. As given, "The heavens declare the glory of God, and the firmament sheweth His handyworks. Day unto day uttereth speech, night unto night sheweth knowledge." This from the beginning and unto the end. [Ps. 19:1, 2] Just in that manner is the way shown how man may escape from all of the fiery darts of the wicked one, for it is self, and selfishness, that would damn the individual soul unto one or the other of those forces that bring about the change that must be in those that willfully wrong his Maker. It is not that which man does or leaves undone, but rather that indifference toward the creation that makes or loses for the individual entity. Then, let's be up and doing—doing—"be ye doers [of the word], and not hearers only". [Jas. 1:22]

Reading 900-20

EC: Yes, we have the conditions here, as would be given from this plane.

As the soul and spirit entity taken its form in the spiritual plane, as the physical body takes form in the material plane, [it is] subject in the spiritual plane to those immutable laws of the spiritual plane. The spiritual entity of the individual composed, then, of the spirit, the superconsciousness, the soul, the subconscious body, as the body prepared for the entity in the spiritual plane, taking then the position in the Universal Force, or space, that the entity has prepared for itself, and goes through its development in that plane, until ready again to manifest in the flesh plane, and sow that degree of development toward that perfection that would make the entity in its entirety perfect, or one with the Creator. This is the cycle, or development, or condition, of the entity in the earth plane, and in the spiritual plane, whether developed to that position to occupy that it occupies, with its relative conditions left in the environment, and giving, partaking, or assisted by such conditions in its completion of development. As this we would find the ever giving forces, as long as not given to becoming in that sphere that would bring the entity into the perfect conjunction with the Universal Force, the entity depending, whether in spiritual plane, or physical plane, upon its relation with the sphere to which it is the closer attracted. Hence we have those conditions as expressed in the earth's plane; those individuals of a spiritual nature, those individuals of the material nature; the nature not changing in its condition, save by the environment of development.

(Q) Are the desires of the earth's plane carried over into the spiritual plane?

(A) When those desires have fastened such hold upon the inner being as to become a portion of the subconsciousness, those desires pass on. Such as one may have in gluttonousness, or in any condition that benumbs the mental forces of the entity, for the subconscious, as given, is the storehouse of every act, thought, or deed. Hence, as we have been given, all are weighed in the balance, as was given in . . . [quotation in Latin]. In these conditions, we find these conditions become a portion of the entity to the extent that the entirety of the subconscious becomes imbibed with that condition, wherein the entity depends upon that element for its sustenance. In such conditions these are carried over. Hence the condition as is seen about such entity having passed into the spirit plane, [it] seeks the gratification of such through the low minded individuals in an earth plane, for as thoughts become deeds, and as such desire is loosed in the plane, such conditions become the taking on of the entity from the sphere, as is given, in that "thoughts are deeds" and live as such.

(Q) Does this mean that our minds on earth plane may be affected by spirit entities, or such desires of the spirit entities, which have carried these desires into the next plane?

(A) Such conditions rely upon the law governing such conditions. When an entity, in the earth plane, desires will manifested to do an error, assisted by error in spirit, as well as in earth plane, as such desire to do that that would assist, they receive hindrances, again they receive the assistance of all good in spirit plane, governed by the law, for law is love, love is law, God is Love.

Reading 262-78

In the beginning God created the heavens and the earth. How? The *mind* of God *moved*, and matter, form, came into being.

Mind, then, in God, the Father, is the builder. How much more, then, would or should Mind be the builder in the experience of those that have put on Christ or God, in Him, in His coming into the earth? For as He has given, "Let that mind be in you which was in the Christ, who thought it not robbery to make Himself equal with God," but living in materiality in the earth, in matter, as a body; but with the Mind, with the thought, with the manifestations of a Creative Force all together.

Then, Destiny as related to that Mind: Mind as related to Destiny must conform, must confine, must be amenable to, must be as one of the immutable laws that has been set by that *mind* calling into being worlds, the universe, the earth, man, giving man a portion of Himself, and furnishing man—as it were—a channel, an access, to that Throne of grace, mercy, truth, that Mind of God itself; the soul, the ultimate, the only portion that may be in accord with or in the presence of Him. For, as has been given, flesh and blood does not inherit eternal life. Flesh and blood is merely an expression, and in all its attributes carries with same those portions, those movements, those urges; just as each atom is made up of urges according to the movement of and with what? That which in its final analysis is the Mind of that Creative Energy which has called into being the mind that is a portion of self. And what is its Destiny? Is it that as the man thinketh in his heart so is he? or as ye sow, so shall ye reap?

That ye think, that ye put your Mind to work upon, to live upon, to feed upon, to live with, to abide with, to associate with in the mind, *that* your soul-body becomes! That is the law. That is the Destiny. That *is* as from the beginning, that each thought of the Creator bore within itself its *own* fruit as from the beginning.

How does matter, how does the seed of the oak or of the grass or of the flower or of the tree or of the animal or of the man, find within itself that which impels, propagates the specie? the activative force that moves on in its realm of activity in whatsoever sphere it may find itself, giving expressions of that first thought of the Creative Forces? That is its Destiny, which the easterners say was set in the first. But, as ye see, this is only half a truth. For if the Mind dwells upon the spiritual things, then it follows that it becomes what it has dwelt upon, what it has lived upon, what it has made itself a portion of. But if the Mind dwells upon self-indulgence, self-aggrandizement, self-exaltation, selfishness in any of its forms, in any of its variations, then it has set itself at variance to that First Cause; and we have that entered in as from the beginning, that of making the will through the Mind—at variance to Creative Forces before it has come into matter, into the movements in matter that we know as physical, material, as those things that are of the earth–earthy.

Yet we find the law, the same law, applying throughout the universe. For what was that which enabled man, or a mind, to first comprehend? "Know, O ye people, the Lord thy God is *one!*" *One* from the beginning to the ending, to those that use, to those that become constructive in their thinking, that are ever constructive in their Minds, in their indwellings, in their resting upon, in their thoughts, in their meditations, and *act in the same manner*, to build towards that which does make, that creates in the experience of each and every soul that knowledge. How easily, then, must it have been said, that it hath not yet entered the mind of man as to the unspeakable glories of him who has washed his raiment in the blood of the Lamb, who has made himself one in thought, in deed, in body, one with that thought, that purpose, that mind, of God.

So as ye contemplate, as ye meditate, as ye look upon the Mind, know the Mind hath many windows. And as ye look out of thine inner self, know whereunto thou art looking, thou art seeking. What is thy ideal? What would you have your mind-body to become? For that upon which it feeds it becomes, that either by thought, by assimilation, by activity, by radial force, by atomic influence, by the very influence of its activity in *whatever sphere* that activity may be within. And in the material mind it is the same.

4

●

Evolution of Body, Mind, and Soul

Reading 900-141 and 900-14

Each and every entity gains its own development, each acting as an individual unit of the Whole, see?(900-141)

. . . In this we find the choice of the spirit's entity, the soul, to choose, with those conditions of like attracting like, bringing itself through the eons of time to the present development, ever being in the form of *man*, God's highest creation in earth's plane, developing through the experiences of the various stages, as given, gaining the knowledge that may at the present time be applied in self's development, and in assistance to others.

Remembering the service to the Creator is giving to His creatures some word of cheer that gives an insight into the development to the realm beyond.

This is evolution.(900-14)

Reading 900-15

(Q) It has been given that the development of the spirit entity of this individual, [900], has reached that point where it has achieved the blessing of this ability to gain the knowledge. Explain and give us the history of this development. Has that development always and only been in the plane of Man? What is meant by plane of Man, as given this body in a reading?

(A) Spirit entity and its development refers not to an earth existence or plane. The development of this spirit entity of [900] refers to its development in the spirit entity in other than an earth plane. The plane of Man refers to the soul and spirit, forming the entity in the human, physical, body in a material world. Do not confuse each development, but consider their co-relation one with the other. Each spirit and soul, the companion of an entity's soul, its spirit, that spark of the Creator, in its passage through the eons of time, or space, developments manifest in the spiritual plane and in an earthly plane. For the attributes of the physical make-up are but the test of the soul's environment, and for its awakening or its development, that it, the soul, may partake of those conditions necessary to develop into such an one as Jesus manifest in the flesh.

(Q) As given, this entity may, if will's forces are correctly used, have no need of further development on earth's plane. Does this mean that the entity may, if it chooses to so live, enter God's Holy of Holies when it leaves earth's plane, or does this mean that the spiritual entity of [900] is merely preparing for another higher plane of eternity, from which development towards God is to continue?

(A) When the conditions as have been outlined and given are considered, this body, this entity, [900], will see, understand, how the present earth's plane so manifests in his self those conditions that would make it possible for him to develop in earth's plane, and so develop in the spiritual plane that the entity would prepare itself, its soul development, of such as would bring it into the realms of the righteous; will's manifestation in the earthly plane being that barrier, for, as has been given, "The spirit is willing, the flesh is weak."

As has been given, God has not willed that *any* should be lost. Man's undoing, then, [is] within himself, by gratifying the desires, the weaknesses of the flesh. Then, as the development of the spiritual entity brings those environments, through which the soul and the earthly entity must pass, or may pass by the relative law of attraction, the will manifests in the earthly sphere, the soul reaching its development by and between the earthly sojourn and its spiritual entity's conditions.

Reading 900-17

(Q) It has also been given in these readings that Jesus lived a man and died a man. It has also been given that God so loved the world as to give His only begotten Son to act as an example, in the flesh, to man. Explain these things to us. How may we regard the truth regarding Jesus in relation to the Jewish and Christian religions, and to all the other religions of the world?

A) In that the man, Jesus, became the ensample of the flesh, manifest in the world, and the will one with the Father, he became the first to manifest same in the material world. Thus, from man's viewpoint, becoming the only, the first, the begotten of the Father, and the ensample to the world, whether Jew, Gentile, or of any other religious forces. In this we find the true advocate with the Father, in that He, as man, manifest in the flesh the ability of the flesh to make fleshly desires one with the will of the spirit. For God is spirit, and they who worship Him must worship in spirit and in truth, just as Jesus manifested in the flesh, and able to partake of the divine, for making all laws susceptible to the mandates. For the will was one with the Father, and in this we find He takes on all law, and a law unto Himself. For with the compliance, of even an earthly or material law, such an person *is* the law. And in that Jesus lived as man, and died as man, and in that became the ensample to all who *would* approach the Throne of God. As we see in all the religions of the world, we find all approaching those conditions where man may become as the law in his connection with the divine, the supreme, the oneness, of the world's manifestation. In Jesus we find the answer.

(Q) It has been given that the soul is the spiritual force that animates or gives life to the body. What is spirit? What is spiritual force? Is it corporeal or incorporeal? Where may we find the soul force in the body—in the brain, nerve centers or where?

(A) There is a vast deal of difference between spiritual and soul forces, for, as given, each force there has been set guards or bounds. Spirit forces are the animation of *all life* giving life-producing forces in animate or inanimate forces. Spiritual elements become corporeal when we speak of the spiritual body in a spiritual entity; then composed of spirit, soul and the superconsciousness. In the soul forces, and its dwelling in man, we find the animation, the spiritual element, the soul that developing element, and contained in the brain, in the nerve, in the centers of the whole system. As to the specific centers, nearer those centers of the sensory system, physically speaking. In the conditions, then, we find when soul and spirit take flight from the animate forces of an human, we find the deadening of all the centers of the sensory system, with the vitality of the solar plexus system, with the gland of the medulla oblongata, these then controlling the forces, and the life becomes extinct, with soul and spirit, with the super-conscious forces, gone. Then, we have as this: Spiritual element, the vitality, produces the motive forces of the entity, whether physical or spiritual. Spiritual forces being the life, the reproductive principle; the soul the development principle. As we have manifested, or illustrated, in the physical body in nerve tissue: There becomes that principle of the nerve action and the nerve in action. That is, with the expression of some condition bringing distress in the body, the active principle is the spirit. The nerve is the soul, for development.

(Q) What happens to the conscious mind forces and physical forces at death?

(A) The conscious mind forces either are in the soul's development, and in the superconsciousness, or left with that portion of material forces which goes to the reclaiming, or remoulding, of physical bodies, for indwelling of spiritual entities.

(Q) Explain universal forces. Are they forces—

(A) (Mr. Cayce, breaking in:) In this, we find that great indwelling of that force as is given in the bounds about all development, whether mental, soul, or spiritual conditions; the universal being that element through which all becomes manifest in a material world, or a spiritual world. As would be illustrated in the prism separating the elements of light, and showing the active principle of given light or heat in its action, by deflection from the given law, the universal forces are as such. These, we see, become manifest in the material world as the mentality of man develops and gains the knowledge of the laws of the universe, and as man in his mentality gains the knowledge of that law, the deflections become the manifestations of universal laws, and force, manifested through the material world. All such laws, as man develops, will come to the use and benefit of man, there being many illustrations in the present age. The greater we find in the life of Jesus, who only used the universal law, and in the deflection of same, through the life lived, made same manifest in the world, in the last overcoming even the disintegration of the spirit and soul from the physical or corporeal body, and able to force all law to become subjugated to the body, or, as we see, manifest in the electrical forces as used by man. This becoming only an atom in motion, and as the atomic force gathers this, producing such vibration as to create heat, light, and of the various natures, by the kind, class or nature of resistance met in its passage in the cycle given, reducing, or raising the velocity, or better by the class of atomic force it vibrates, either with or against. These are ensamples of portions of universal forces.

Reading 900-23

(Q) Give us the relation of evolution and thought transferences. How may thought transference be developed?

(A) Just as has been described, when related to many individuals, we find that when thought of many individuals are directed to one focusing point, the condition becomes accentuated by force—see?—of thought manifested. In evolution, we find the development as has been just given, in the correlation of the human mind and soul, toward perfection. Just so the evolution of the soul came in the attributes of God Mind, and given in Man. As thoughts are directed, the transmission of thought waves gradually becomes the reality, just as light and heat waves in material world are now used by man. Just to in the spiritual planes, the elements of thought transmission, or transference, may become real. Be sure of this fact, and assured of same. Thought transference occurs when both bodies, or entities, are in the subconscious condition, whether for a moment, or whether for ages, for time in spiritual forces is not as in material forces.

Reading 900-249

(Q) Explain in the light of inheritance and evolution, in line with that I am now writing on that subject.

(A) That's just given. Follow that line—for there may be much said as respecting this condition, for in this force and in this manifestation of the material world, and of the creative energy as is manifested, is the stumbling block to many peoples, for evolution is as of a fact in the mind of the creative energy, and the will of the energy creating is of the higher forces, same as the will of the individual in the higher species, or as in man in propagating species, yet there may be those physical conditions as existing which prevent such propagation, see? with the will manifested correctly, yet there may exist that physical condition within the body which prevents such conditions taking place, yet the species may be propagated through that variation, and the variation or the acceptance of the condition is the proof of the heredity, of the environmental conditions, and not a disproval of the spirit forces as manifesting in the material world, for the same germinate (?) [germinative] condition exists in the species of the higher creation as of the lower creation, for the motive energy is from the divine, and is to that consciousness as has attained to that consciousness of the higher dimension, or of the higher evolution of mind within species as to see that this condition existing is the manifestation, literal, spiritual, physical being of the manifestation of the divine forces in the material world.

Reading 699-1

For, as has been in the experience, and as is partially understood by the entity, everything in motion, everything that has taken on materiality as to become expressive in any kingdom in the material world, is *by* the *vibrations* that are the motions—or those positive and negative influences that make for that differentiation that man has called matter in its various stages of evolution into material things. For it enters and it passes through. For—as is the better understood, and as will be proclaimed (and the entity may be able to aid in same)—all vibration must eventually, as it materializes into matter, pass through a stage of evolution and out. For it rises in its emanations and descends also. Hence the cycle, or circle, or arc, that is as a description of all influence in the experience of man. And very few do they come at angles!

Reading 3744-3

(Q) Is memory thought, or thought memory?

(A) With the evolving of the individual, the thought becomes a part of the memory as evolved through the developing of the entity. In memory, we may have either plane, in physical or mental speaking—they are separate. In that of spirit and soul forces, thought and memory depending then upon the plane from which the question is approached. Physically, memory and thought are not synonymous, neither are they of the same beginning in physical forces. In that of the soul and spirit force, they become one and the same in evolution.

(Q) In the physical plane, do the thoughts of another person affect a person either mentally or physically?

(A) Depending upon the development of the individual to whom the thought may be directed. The possibilities of the developing of thought transference is first being shown, evolution, you see. The individuals of this plane will and are developing this as the senses were and are developed.

Reading 1947-3

The body finds itself Body, Mind and Soul; the body with all its attributes, with the mental and material and physical desires and emotions; the mental with its hopes and fears, its aspirations and desires; the spiritual with its longings, its wonderments, its interpreting of the emotions of physical and mental being.

These, then, in the light of all that has been indicated, should be analyzed, and then the premise from which the ideal is to be drawn; and how same works with the *entity* as an entity.

It has already been indicated in the information given that the entity has abilities in certain directions, partaking of the mental and spiritual or soul forces; as well as much to be met in the physical emotions.

Mind is the builder; it is both spiritual and physical, and thus has its aspirations, its limitations, its fears, its hopes, its desires.

To determine, then, whether the emotions or influences which arise from one experience to another are from purely a mental aspiration of a physical desire, or from a spiritual aspect and hope in its relationships to the things desired of self, comparisons need to be drawn for the entity as to how, and in what manner judgments or choices are to be made.

The body finds itself Body, Mind, Soul; just as seen in that after which it is patterned—Father, Son, Holy Spirit.

In the choices, then, it is seen that each of these phases of spiritual experience finds its own place of activity, as illustrated in the entity's experience in materiality.

The *Spirit* moved—or soul moved—and there was Light (Mind). The Light became the light of men—Mind made aware of conscious existence in spiritual aspects or relationships as one to another.

The mind in the entity becomes aware of longings, innate in the inner self; also the arousing of emotions in the physical attributes of the body—just as indicated as to how these came into *being*; as self is a part of Creative Forces or God, Spirit, the Son. These are one. The body, mind and soul are one. Their desires must be one; their purposes, their aims must be one—then—to be ideal.

What, then, has this to do with the entity in its seeking for the use of its own abilities in the psychic, the mental, the material atmosphere in which it finds itself in the present?

There are laws, then, as govern the physical, the mental, the spiritual body, and the attributes of each of these. The abuse of a physical law brings dis-ease and then disturbance to the physical organism, through which mental and spiritual portions of the body operate.

There are also promises, warnings, and governing forces, as has been indicated, for the physical and the mental and spiritual being—as given by those forces and influences which manifest in the material world as respecting each of these.

As the Mind indicated, "I and the Father are one; he that abideth in me as I abide in the Father *hath* eternal life." Not *will* have, not *may* have, but *hath*—now—is in eternal consciousness of being at a onement with eternal influence and force!

And this is the moving of the spirit that has brought and does bring life, light, to the consciousness of the entity in whatever phase of experience it may be passing.

Then how, in what manner, does one accomplish such? Not by thoughts of self. If God had not given free will to man, or the children of men, would they have been able to be equal with Him? Rather would they be as the natural sources of the universal consciousness of group vibration—as is indicated about the entity.

"Be not deceived," then, it was given, "God is not mocked; whatsoever a man soweth, that must he also reap."

Then, not merely by *doing* does the awareness come, but by *being in* the doing does the awareness come of the relationships as one portion of body, mind and soul finds.

These then grow, as indicated, as do individuals. This entity as an entity grows in grace, in knowledge, in understanding.

As was indicated, the body was first a cell by the union of desire that brought activity in that influence about which the growth began.

Then of itself at birth into materiality the consciousness gradually awoke to the influences about same of body, mind and soul, until it reached the consciousness of the ability for the reproduction within itself of desire, hope, fear.

And the whole of creation, then, is bound in the consciousness of self. That influence, that force is the psychic self.

As to how same, then, may be developed within self:

Each entity enters materiality for a purpose. That all the experiences in the earth are as one is indicated by the desires, the longings as arise within the experience of that which makes for the growing, the knowing within self—*Mind!* Thus does the entity, as a whole, become aware that it, itself, in body, mind and soul, is the result—each day—of the application of laws pertaining to creation, this evolution, this soul-awareness within, consciously manifested.

What is the purpose of entering consciousness? That each phase of body, mind and soul may be to the glory of that Creative Force in which it moves and has its being.

And when this influence, this growing self becomes such, or so self-centered, as to lose sight of that desire, purpose, aim to be *to* the glory of its source, and seeks rather *for* self, then it errs in its application of the influences within its abilities for the application of mind within its own experience.

Thus we find this entity capable of arousing others, or of becoming the incentive to and the motivative force of many—in and through its application of itself in the material world; as a worshipful experience to that something within the entity itself which magnifies—by the reflections—the awareness of the attributes of body, mind and soul in the experiences of others.

Hence the great intuitive forces, the abilities to raise the vibratory influence within the lives and the experiences of others through the use or the application of those abilities within their own selves—these become a part of the entity's experience; mentally first, and it grows either to that of materiality, material desire, or to those influences that are creative, constructive, spiritual in their nature.

Those things then as may be aroused by the self, by this entity, within the experiences of those it meets—either in close association or in casual meeting—may either create something that is material (which means only temporal), or something that is spiritual, that is eternal.

Then, as has been said: There is before thee this day life and death, good and evil. These are the ever present warring influences within materiality.

What then, ye ask, is this entity to do about, to do with, this ability of its own spiritual or psychic development; that may be made creative or may bring creative or destructive forces within the experiences of others?

"My Spirit beareth witness with thy spirit as to whether ye be the children of God or not." This becomes, then, that force, that influence for comparisons; as the entity meditates upon its own emotions, its own influences, these become very apparent within itself for comparisons.

Do they bespeak of kindness, gentleness, patience,—that threshold upon which godliness appears?

Desire may be godly or ungodly, dependent upon the purpose, the aim, the emotions aroused.

Does it bring, then, self-abstinence? or does it bring self-desire?

Does it bring love? Does it bring longsuffering? Is it gentle? Is it kind?

Then, these be the judgments upon which the entity uses those influences upon the lives of others.

Does it relieve suffering, as the abilities of the entity grow? Does it relieve the mental anguish, the mental disturbances which arise? Does it bring also healing—of body, of mind, to the individual? Is it healed for constructive force, or for that as will bring pain, sorrow, hate and fear into the experience of others?

These be the judgments upon which the entity makes its choices, as it guides, directs or gives counsel to those who are seeking—seeking—What? That Light—which has become, which is, which ever was the light of the world!

What was that light? The Spirit of God moved, and there *was* light! That Light came—the light of men, yea, dwelt among men as *Mind* with the ability to choose, the ability to abstain, the ability to put away desire, hate, fear, and to put on the whole armor. All of these are attributes then of those influences and forces which are a part of the entity's experience.

And as these are applied, so may the entity come to apply its psychic abilities, its love, its desire, its hopes, *spiritualized* in self-effacement by placing God's *glory*, God's *love*, in the place of self; bringing hope, *hope* and *faith* in the minds and hearts, the lives of others.

This is the mission of the entity in this experience; fulfilling much of that sought after, much of that at times lost in self-desire. But often seeking, knowing, applying, ye become closer and closer in an at-one-ment with Him.

These are the purposes, these are the desires, these are the manners in which the mental may be applied for the soul and spiritual development; and in the manner, "As ye do it to the least of these, thy brethren, ye do it unto me," saith the Lord.

Ready for questions.

(Q) Please give detailed directions for the entity regarding her mental and spiritual development through meditation. Outline the steps she should take that best fit her development.

(A) First—as was indicated to those of old—purge or purify thy body—whether this be by mental means or by ablutions, do it in that manner as to satisfy thine own conscience. Then, enter into the holy of holies of thine own inner self; for there He hath promised to meet thee. Let thy prayer be as this: "As I surround myself with the consciousness of the Christ-Mind, may I—in body, in purpose, in desire—be purified to become the channel through which He may *direct* me in that *He*, the Christ, would have me do;" as respecting an individual, a condition, an experience. And as ye wait on Him, the answer will come. Then each day *live*, towards those ye meet, in the same manner as ye prayed.

Reading 5753–1 [Entire reading]

GC: You will give at this time a comprehensive discourse on reincarnation. If the soul returns to the earth through a succession of appearances, you will explain why this is necessary or desirable and will clarify through explanation the laws governing such returns. You will answer the questions which will be asked on this subject.

EC: Yes. In giving even an approach to the subject sought here, it is well that there be given some things that may be accepted as standards from which conclusions—or where parallels—may be drawn, that there may be gathered in the minds of those who would approach same some understanding, some concrete examples, that may be applied in their own individual experience.

Each soul that enters, then, must have had an impetus from some beginning that is of the Creative Energy, or of a first cause.

What, then, was—or is—the first cause; for if there be law pertaining to the first cause it must be an unchangeable law, and is—is—as "I am that I am!" For this is the basis from which one would reason:

The first cause was, that the created would be the companion for the Creator; that it, the creature, would—through its manifestations in the activity of that given unto the creature—show itself to be not only worthy of, but companionable to, the Creator.

Hence, every form of life that man sees in a material world is an essence or manifestation of the Creator; not the Creator, but a manifestation of a first cause—and in its own sphere, its own consciousness of its activity in that plane or sphere.

Hence, as man in this material world passes through, there are the manifestations of the attributes that the consciousness attributes to, or finds coinciding with, that activity which is manifested; hence becomes then as the very principle of the law that would govern an entrance into a manifestation.

Then a soul, the offspring of a Creator, entering into a consciousness that became a manifestation in any plane or sphere of activity, given that free-will for its use of those abilities, qualities, conditions in its experience, demonstrates, manifests, shows forth, that it reflects in its activity towards that first cause.

Hence in the various spheres that man sees (that are demonstrated, manifested, in and before self) even in a material world, all forces, all activities, are a manifestation. Then, that which would be the companionable, the at-oneness with, the ability to be one with, becomes necessary for the demonstration or manifestation of those attributes in and through all force, all demonstration, in a sphere.

Because an atom, a matter, a form, is changed does not mean that the essence, the source or the spirit of it has changed; only in its form of manifestation, and *not* in its relation with the first cause. That man reaches that consciousness in the material plane of being aware of what he does about or with the consciousness of the knowledge, the intelligence, the first cause, makes or produces that which is known as the entering into the first cause, principles, basis, or the essences, that there may be demonstrated in that manifested that which gains for the soul, for the entity, that which would make the soul an acceptable companion to the Creative Force, Creative Influence. See?

As to how, where, when, and what produces the entrance into a material manifestation of an entity, a soul:

In the beginning was that which set in motion that which is seen in manifested form with the laws governing same. The inability of destroying matter, the ability of each force, each source of power or contact—as it meets in its various forms, produces that which is a manifestation in a particular sphere. This may be seen in those elements used in the various manifested ways of preparing for man, in many ways, those things that bespeak of the laws that govern man's relationship to the first cause, or God.

Then, this is the principle:

Like begets like. Those things that are positive and negative forces combine to form in a different source, or different manifestation, the combinations of which each element, each first principle manifested, has gained from its associations—in its activities—that which has been brought to bear by self or that about it, to produce that manifestation.

Hence man, the crowning of all manifestations in a material world—a causation world, finds self as the cause and the product of that he (man), with those abilities given, has been able to produce, or demonstrate, or manifest from that he (the soul) has gained, does gain, in the transition, the change, the going toward that (and being of that) from which he came.

Periods, times, places: That which is builded, each in its place, each in its time.

This is shown to man in the elemental world about him. Man's consciousness of that about him is gained through that he, man, does about the knowledge of that he is, as in relation to that from which he came and towards which he is going.

Hence, in man's analysis and understanding of himself, it is as well to know from whence he came as to know whither he is going.

Ready for questions.

(Q) What is meant by inequality of experience? Is it a strong argument for reincarnation?

(A) Considering that which has just been presented, isn't it the same argument?

(Q) Is experience limited to this earth plane?

(A) As each entity, each soul, in the various consciousnesses, passes from one to another, it—the soul—becomes conscious of that about self in that sphere—to which it, the entity, the soul attains in a materially manifested way or manner. Hence the entity develops *through* the varied spheres of the earth and its solar system, and the companions of varied experiences in that solar system, or spheres of development or activity; as in some ways accredited correctly to the planetary influences in an experience. The entity develops *through* those varied spheres. Hence the sun, the moon, the stars, the position in the heavens or in all of the hosts of the solar systems that the earth occupies—all have their influence in the same manner (this is a very crude illustration, but very demonstrative) that the effect of a large amount of any element would attract a compass. Drawn to! Why? Because of the influence of which the mind element of a soul, an entity, has become conscious! A soul, an entity, is as real as a physical entity, and is as subject to laws as the physical body as subject to the laws in a material world and the elements thereof! Does fire burn the soul or the physical body? Yet, self may cast self into a fire element by doing that the soul knows to be wrong! What would make a wrong and a right? A comparison of that the soul knows its consciousness to be in accord or contrarywise with, in relation to that which gave it existence.

(Q) Are not transferred memories misappropriated by individuals and considered to be personal experiences?

(A) Personal experiences have their influence upon the inner soul, while disincarnate entities (that may be earth-bound, or that may be heaven-bound) may influence the thought of an entity or a mind. But, who gives the law to have an element to influence, whether from self or from others? That same as from the beginning. The *will* of the soul that it may be one with the first cause. In the material, the mental, and the spiritual experience of many souls, many entities, it has been found that there *be* those influences that *do* have their effect upon the thought of those that would do this or that. Who gives it? Self! Just as it is when an entity, a body, fills its mind (mentally, materially) with those experiences that bespeak of those things that add to the carnal forces of an experience. Just so does the mind become the builder throughout. And the mental mind, or physical mind, becomes *carnally* directed! The mind is the builder ever, whether in the spirit or in the flesh. If one's mind is filled with those things that bespeak of the spirit, that one becomes spiritual-minded. As we may find in a material world: Envy, strife, selfishness, greediness, avarice, are the children of *man*! Long-suffering, kindness, brotherly love, good deeds, are the children of the spirit of light. Choose ye (as it has ever been given) whom ye will serve. This is not beggaring the question! As individuals become abased, or possessed, are their thoughts guided by those in the borderland? Certainly! If allowed to be! But he that looks within is higher, for the spirit knoweth the Spirit of its Maker—and the children of same are as given. And, "My Spirit beareth witness with thy spirit," saith He that giveth life! What *is* Life? A manifestation of the first cause—God!

(Q) Explain, in the light of reincarnation, the cycle of development towards maturity in individuals.

(A) As an individual in any experience, in any period, uses that of which it (the soul or entity) is conscious in relation to the laws of the Creative Forces, so does that soul, that entity, develop towards—what? A companionship with the Creative influence! Hence karma, to those disobeying—by making for self that which would be as the towers of Babel, or as the city of Gomorrah, or as the fleshpots of Egypt, or as the caring for those influences in the experience that satisfy or gratify self without thought of the effect upon that which it has in its own relation to the first cause! Hence to many this becomes as the stumblingblock. It is as was given by Him, "I am the way. No man approaches the Father but by me." But, does a soul crucify the flesh even as He, when it finds within itself that it must work out its own salvation in a material world, by entering and re-entering that there may be made manifest that consciousness in the soul that would make it a companion with the Creator? Rather is the law of forgiveness made of effect in thine experience, through Him that would stand in thy stead; for He is the way, that light ever ready to aid when there is the call upon—and the trust of the soul in—that first cause! Has it not been given that there *is* an influence in the mind, the thought of man, from the outside? Then, would those that have lost their way become the guides and both fall in the ditch? or would the soul trust in the Way, and the Light, and seek in that way that there may be shown the light? What caused the first influences in the earth that brought selfishness? The desire to be as gods, in that rebellion became the order of the mental forces in the soul; and sin entered.

(Q) What is the strongest argument against reincarnation?

(A) That there is the law of cause and effect in *material* things. But the strongest argument against reincarnation is also, turned over, the strongest argument for it; as in *any* principle, when reduced to its essence. For the *law* is set—and it happens! though a soul may will itself *never* to reincarnate, but must burn and burn and burn—or suffer and suffer and suffer! For, the heaven and hell is built by the soul! The companionship in God is being one with Him; and the gift of God is being conscious of being one with Him, yet apart from Him—or one with, yet apart from, the Whole.

(Q) What is the strongest argument for reincarnation?

(A) Just as given. Just turn it over; or, as we have outlined.

Reading 892–1

First in self find what are the promptings for thy activities, in relationships to thy fellow man. Know thy ideal; not of mental or material import but of the spiritual. For *Mind* is the builder, the Spirit is the motivative force and is the turning of self to the things of the spirit; then may the promptings make for that in the experience in whatever direction the activities may be taken, to be of a *constructive* nature in the experience of the entity. And only these bring peace, harmony, joy of life, of service, of activity.

Reading 263–13

GC: You will have before you the body and the enquiring mind of [263], present in this room, the information which has been given through these channels in her [263-4] Life Reading on March 6, 1935, as to her appearances in the earth and how they effect the physical and mental body in the present. You will answer the questions, as I ask them:

EC: Yes, we have the body, the enquiring mind, [263], present in this room; together with the information respecting influences which arise in the mental and material body from urges in past sojourns.

These in part, and wholly in some, we have had before.

In analyzing the conditions–physical and mental that exist in the present, all of these—with the present material happenings and experiences—are to be considered as a whole, yet analyzed in such a way and manner that the suggestions for help or aid may be made practical in the experience.

Hence, first, in the physical forces of the body:

Let it be understood as to how each phase of consciousness or experience affects the other; that is, the associations or connections between the spiritual and the mental body, the spiritual and the physical body, and between the mental and the physical and mental and spiritual.

Thus, if these associations and connections are thoroughly understood—as to the manners and the means then of controlling emotions, whether they be physical, mental or spiritual, may be better understood and applied in the experience of the entity.

As has been indicated through these channels respecting that which takes place at the moment of conception, as to ideals and purposes of those who through physical and mental emotions bring into being a channel through which there may be the expression of a soul-entity—each soul choosing such a body at the time of its birth into material activity has its physical being controlled much by the environs of the individuals responsible for the physical entrance. Yet, the soul choosing such a body for a manifestation becomes responsible for that temple of the living God, when it has developed in body, in mind, so as to be controlled with intents, purposes and desires of the individual entity or soul.

So in this body, in this physical condition that exists here with this body, [263], we find it subject to those attributes of a physical being it has chosen for the mental and soul expression of self.

Then, there are centers, areas, conditions in which there evidently must be that contact between the physical, the mental and spiritual.

The spiritual contact is through the glandular forces of creative energies; not encased only within the [Leydig] lyden gland of reproduction, for this is ever—so long as life exists—in contact with the brain cells through which there is the constant reaction through the pineal.

Hence we find these become subject not only to the intent and purpose of the individual entity or soul upon entrance, but are constantly under the influences of *all* the centers of the mind *and* the body through which the impulses pass in finding a means or manner of expression in the mental or brain self.

This is true also in regard to physical ills that have been a part of an individual experience; as this entity has had through the periods of development, the periods of satisfaction and gratification of the emotions of the body in all its phases of experience, as well as in the building through the mental self that which is the experience of the entity.

Thus we find the connection, the association of the spiritual being with the mental self, at those centers from which the reflexes react to all of the organs, all of the emotions, all of the activities of a physical body.

That this individual body in the mental, in the spiritual, in the present sojourn, has experienced illness, dis–ease rather than disease, has had and does in the present have an influence upon the abilities of the entity to choose or to facilitate itself in its environs. Not that there has been or is a lack of appreciation, or a lack of knowledge as to what may be done by physical activity or mental attitudes towards spiritual influences. But being *physically* submerged by the conditions and experiences which have over-shadowed the body-mind as well as the physical reflexes and activities to the mental forces as to the creative influences within the body, there remains that ability of the entity itself to keep that emotion—as it were—*aflame* with the desire to carry on. For, the mental and physical pressures that have been so strong upon the spiritual-mental attitude have the tendency to submerge.

Hence, as indicated at times, and as outlined for the body in the urges arising from the sojourns in other periods when there were the expressions of self-emotions, self-indulgence, followed by the periods of self-condemnation—these conditions that exist in the present would or might be expected to arise. For, the tendencies are for the physical body to gradually conform to that which has been the experience of the entity in other activities, as to what it did *about* those periods of physical and mental activity with a disregard of the spiritual influences. These become latent urges, and gradually build such a body. For, that a body—this body—assimilates, it is able to be added to the physical being, the mental being, the spiritual being. It is dependent then upon those abilities within each entity to keep alive, to keep aware of, to keep aglow that which is the life impelling force or hope, against despair or willfulness, against contentment.

These are mental or deeper expressions of emotions,—until an individual entity has grasped hold of such as to make the awareness of same real.

How? All being of one accord, moved to this or that activity! Or better—in the beginning was the word. The word was God. The word was with God. He *moved!*

Hence as He moved, souls—portions of Himself—came into being.

This entity—as a portion—may come to the awareness then of its relationship to that source, that glow or impulse of life. Separation or willfulness or neglect may bring just the opposite—disappointment, fear, contention, strife, the inclination of discontent in *any* factor, in *any* influence.

These, then, are conditions that exist; mentally, spiritually, physically, with this body.

Now: As has been indicated, there is that existent influence; that He, the Father, has not willed that any soul should perish. He does not have joy in suffering, in death, in disappointment, in hate, in those things that make individual souls or entities afraid, but has with *all* the willfulness of an entity, a soul, prepared a way of escape. For, was not the physical being made from all else that grew? For, of the dust of the earth was the body–physical created. But the *word*, the *Mind*, is the controlling factor of its shape, its activity, from the source, the spiritual—the spiritual entity.

Thus there are within the abilities of each soul that ability to choose that as will keep the body, the mind, the portion of the spirit, attuned to holiness—or oneness with him.

Reading 262–56

(Q) [288]: Is it true that day and night are condensed or miniature copies of incarnations into the earth and into planetary or spiritual sojourns; they in turn being miniature copies of what took place in the Beginning?

(A) Very good, if you understood just what all this means! It's a very good illustration of that which has just been given; as to how there is the evolution of the soul, evolution of the mind, but not evolution of matter—save through mind, and that which builds same.

Reading 2454–4

From the advent of the souls of man into materiality, laws were initiated; such as is evidenced by the psalmist, "The heavens declare the glory of God, the firmament sheweth his handiwork; day unto day uttereth speech, night unto night sheweth his handiwork." And yet how oft might each soul cry out, "*Why* art Thou, O God, mindful of the spirit of man, when he stumbleth so blindly and hateth his brother?"

This would indicate, then, that God in His love and His mercy hath given to man that with which the individual may exalt His name in the earth. And as He hath from days of old, He has given those examples in the seers and prophets,—yea in this latter day hath He spoken more direct through His Son. Yet these are self-evident facts:

Man's destiny lies within his individual grasp, doth he take hold upon those laws, those self-evident truths. Applying them in his relationships one to another there may come the knowledge that He walketh and talketh with those who would, who do, exalt and glorify His name in the earth.

Man is hedged about by beliefs, by cults, by schisms, by isms—yes. And those things have been created by man that he hath given power in themselves to rule his days. Yet this is only because man has given them such power. For the spirit of truth and wisdom is mighty, and a bulwark of faith and hope to those that trust in Him. But they that give others, other things, power over themselves become subject unto them. Thus hath He declared, as was given of Him who is the way, the truth and the light, the first, yea the whole of the commandment of the Lord is encompassed in this: "Thou shalt have no other god before me, neither in heaven nor in earth, nor in things seen or unseen, but thou shalt love the Lord thy God with all thine heart, thine soul and thine body, and thy neighbor as thyself."

5

●

Jesus as an Evolutionary Pattern

Reading 2067-7

(Q) When did the knowledge come to Jesus that he was to be the Savior of the world?

(A) When he fell in Eden.

Reading 2533-7

(Q) What is the meaning and significance of the words Jesus and Christ as should be understood and applied by these entities in the present?

(A) Just as indicated. Jesus is the man—the activity, the mind, the relationships that He bore to others. Yea, He was mindful of friends, He was sociable, He was loving, He was kind, He was gentle. He grew faint, He grew weak—and yet gained that strength that He has promised, in becoming the Christ, by fulfilling and overcoming the world! Ye are made strong—in body, in mind, in soul and purpose—by that power in Christ. The *power*, then, is in the Christ. The *pattern* is in Jesus.

Reading 2067-1

As to the appearances in the earth—these, as indicated, are many; they have varied much as to their forces and powers, as to how the emotions have manifested. For, as must be the proper interpretation of same,—material sojourns are as the senses of the material body, just as the astrological sojourns are as the mental or dream body. Thus they find expression oft in *feelings* towards places, conditions, individuals, that in thine own inner self send out that radiation which (in mystical study) may be seen in the aura, or in the study of a part of numerology as to the number, or in the very emotions as may be expressed in lines of the hand, feet or face. For, remember the law—all carry the mark in their body; just as ye bear His mark in thy forehead.

In these manners, then—oft in the emotions being five rather than the three (as the earth is interpreted as a three-dimensional sphere of activity), we come to the realm through such emotions or senses—of the fourth, yea and to the fifth dimension. Thus the warning that has been given,—that because of such emotions in self ye will find others oft question thy authority, because of thy interpreting of fourth or fifth dimensional experiences and expressing same in three-dimensional terms!

Only those who know God or have sought Him may interpret even His walks among men!

So, be mindful—as He warned Thomas, Philip, Andrew and Peter, as well as showed to James and John, that these things are oft hard to be understood by those who may only know that which answers to the sensuousness-consciousness of an entity. Not the senses as the higher realm, but sensuousness that begets (and its children are!) lasciviousness and those forces that engorge or indulge in those things that gratify appetites, and those things that become a part of many who become self-indulgent in habit forming, habit creating.

For, the animal man is a creature of habit. But learn rather from such the lesson, and not become so much a part of same. For in nature and in the animal instincts we find only the expressions of a universal consciousness of hope, and never of fear—save created by man in his indulging in the gratification of material appetites.

Before this we find the entity was in the land of the present nativity, during the early experiences in the land, when there were the questionings as to those forces, powers, mandates and acts about Salem and Provincetown.

Then in the name Dorothy Manley, the entity suffered much for a just cause; misunderstood, misinterpreted. For the voices as heard, the movements as experienced, even as a young girl, were hounded by those who understood not.

Learn ye then that lesson in the present, "Cast not pearls before dogs nor swine." For as the dog returns to his vomit and the hog to his wallow, so will they that listen at pearls of great price yet have no thought, no mind, no purpose for same.

In the experience the entity found material hardships, mental satisfaction, spiritual awakening; and thus gained in all phases of its experience through that sojourn.

The entity was young in years when it lost its experience through the so oft being dipped, as to contract that known in the present as pneumonia—and passed in a high fever.

In the present such has been the experience of the entity, to catch a glimpse oft, under similar circumstances, from and in various fields of activity, of a something that has taken hold upon self. Remember—these are shadows, and that the real is in Him.

Before that the entity was in the land [Palestine] of the Master of masters' sojourn in the earth.

During those periods the entity was a queen of no mean estate, and took hold upon the words of the Master—though never personally coming in contact with Him. For the entity then was the companion or wife of Herod, who sought His destruction. Yet the entity's experience there, as Thesea, sought a closer comprehending of the Wise Men.

Thus the entity will, or may in this experience find, even by the conversation with one of these—that is in the city of its own birth—the interpretations of those experiences and periods that brought about the determinations to cry out, as it did, that brought material or physical extinction—and bore in its activity the very same influences and forces that were upon the minds of many by Calvary.

For as the entity reasoned with the Essenes, as well as conversed with the Wise Men who came with the new messages to the world, the entity proclaimed—yea, that pronouncement that He Himself then being announced had given—"Others may do as they may, but as for me and my house, we will serve the living God."

Do not interpret this to mean those who may be in thine own physical household. Thy house is indeed thy body,—*that* is the temple of the living God. *That* is the whole house made to conform to the will, the way. "He that loves me keeps my commandments," in body, in mind, in soul.

Reading 3132-1

The material is of the earth-earthy. The spiritual is of the heavenly or the motivative forces. The mental is ever the builder.

Then, apply self in the spiritual imports of tenets or truths that comply with the universal consciousness for the greater material benefits in the material plane.

That as would be manifested must first be in spirit, then in mind, then in material activity. For, this is the evolution of the earth, the evolution of things, the evolution of ideas and of ideals. For, He came into the earth that through Him man might have access again to the grace and mercy of those spiritual forces that are the directing ideals of each soul-entity.

Reading 900-100 (Entire reading)

GC: You will have before you the reading [900-89] taken on [900] on July 7, 1925, regarding the one spirit being the elemental force or cause of everything, and man's relation to this great creative force. You will also have previous readings given, in which it gave Jesus as an ensample to all in physical, and you will answer the following questions, correcting any statement not properly stated.

EC: Yes, we have the reading here, the information regarding same and co-relating influences as were and are manifest to man in the life of Jesus in the earth plane, co-relating and making man, through Him, one with the Father, God, becoming then One with Him, through having passed through man's plane of existence, being the whole interpretation of the Gift of God to man, and the highest in the evolution of man in earth's plane being one with man, One with God. The propitiation for the sin of man in that He *shows* the way, and through following that way man becomes One with Him. Ready for questions.

(Q) "As given, 'We are God, that Spirit Father, performing our functions as portions, yet capable of becoming perfect like that whole spirit and absorbing the power of the Whole.' Then Jesus Christ like us was man, but made perfect as the Whole spirit and so became equal to or One with the Whole Spirit Father."

(A) Correct.

(Q) "Jesus was a man until development brought him to one with God? We, each and everyone of us, may according to our heritage, become likewise. Is this true? Is this not the meaning of the Bible where it says, 'We are all heirs with Christ to the Kingdom.'"

(A) This is a physical, literal, interpretation of that passage as given. In that Christ Jesus came into the world as the representation of the Father, in the flesh, this then the portion (as man), for this in the evolution, the evolving, the resuscitation, the presentation of the God Spirit manifest through the living forces as are in the world become carnate in the man Jesus. He, the Son of God and through Him man heir to the Kingdom of God, the Creator; then representing in flesh the creation of Him who becomes the heir, and we are heirs with him.

(Q) "Jesus was made perfect, God come into His Own. We are man not yet perfect, God not yet equal to God. He represents our so-called future, the path to the Throne."

(A) Correct. He is the path to the throne, in that we, man, must become as the One as directs the way.

(Q) "Only by fourth dimension logic may this be comprehended. Can be both that and not that. Like us, Jesus was both God and Man until he became God alone."

(A) Correct.

(Q) "Jesus exemplifies that which I am studying, that is, Man is that portion of the Whole Spirit which may acquire the power and equality with the Whole Spirit, God."

(A) Correct.

(Q) "Then God's Kingdom is our Kingdom. We are It and in It we may acquire power, wisdom, and the Throne."

(A) Only through *It* do we acquire power or wisdom. The compliance with the laws of the Creator, His forces as are manifest in the world. Whether of Spirit, Flesh or Mind, all are under subjugation of those powers, same as were made manifest in the Son when He overcame all, for as we find, this is the dominant question in the questions as asked:

In Christ Jesus (Man), we find Him Son of man, born of woman, in the flesh, in a material world. Entering, then, in the material world in flesh, He becomes the Son of Man. In His first compliance with the physical laws, separating Him from man's so thinking, or man's status [stature?

status?] of thinking, we have the exemplification of the recognition of His being the Son of God. As each and every individual acquires within that answer, "My spirit beareth witness with your spirit" (God speaking to man), whether ye be the Sons of God or not, see? In the full compliance of these laws, he becomes *fully* (All are Sons of God), He becomes *fully* the Son, as He was in the Beginning, with the ever present condition of earth, with all its earthly callings and environments, its snares, its entrapments, its every force being exercised, overcoming *all* in making His *will one with the Father.*

We are through.

Reading 900-147

(Q) Saw Rabbi Wise* in pulpit and recalled his lectures on Christ—particularly those admitting Christ to be a perfect man—but not a God. I seemed to want to get up on that platform. Awakening then I found myself reasoning as though continuing right on from dream: Christ represents the Evolution of this Spirit Energy into Flesh Man—the Perfect Flesh Man, Wise concedes. Then (again that last phase as indicated in first dream) Christ's evolution to His present Spiritual Omnipotence—Spiritual Oneness with the Whole Spirit Force (not an all powerful individual man floating around spirit like in the atmosphere or somewheres in the heavens) but an energy capable of acting here—there—everywhere throughout the realm (all power over Heaven and Earth) but a *self conscious intelligent rational Energy*—a 4th dimension Energy fully evolved—such is God.

(A) Correct. * [GD's note: Rabbi Stephen Samuel Wise, founder of Zionist Organization of America, etc., etc., etc., whose monthly sermons in various synagogues were available in published volumes. See WHO'S WHO in 1924-1925.]

(Q) Is this a revelation—a revelation of that I was pondering—what is meant by Life Eternal?

(A) Life Eternal—One with that Oneness, as is seen by the Soul becoming One with the Will, the spirit, of the Father, even as is shown in the ensample of the Man called Jesus—the Christ, the Savior of the World, through compliance to those same laws, as He complied with, see? for with that Force, that Spirit, brought in the World, then becomes the truth, "What thou asketh in My name, believing in thine heart, same shall be unto thee." *Beautiful* is the life and the feet of those who walk in the paths of the righteous One. Lo! The Heavens open and I see Him stand at that Way which leads unto Life Everlasting; *that* then the Way, the Truth, the Light, the Water of Life, the Man made Perfect in that Spirit of Him who gave Himself as the ransom for many. In this is the ransom then: Making self of low estate, as is called in man's realm. All power-ful—yet never using that power, save to help, to assist, to give aid, to give succor to someone who is not in that position to help or aid self, see?

(Q) Again and again and again trying to make me see the scope, the wide meaning of "All of These are God."

(A) All of these are God, manifesting in the Spirit to those who would seek His face, see?

Reading 900–233

(Q) Voice: "Have a trial balance."

(A) This again a presentation of the conditions in which the entity is rather to bring a trial balance with these conditions as have been pre-sented, rather than that of a trial balance as respecting books or ledger, see? A trial balance here is, as we see, from the subconscious mind again reasoning or answering the conditions in the body consciousness of the individual, and is, as it were, giving this: As the entity draws, materially, trial balances for the conditions as are gained, lost, or as these physical conditions for the gain of the material body are seen by the drawing of the trial balance, so may the body consciousness draw within self those very conditions which the entity has been reasoning, as it were, with self—a trial balance of *what* has been the *gain* by the entity in the study of self, in the study of those conditions that represent the manifestations of spirit force in the material world; *what* do these mean materially to the entity now? Have these become as a loss, or are these as a gain? and the entity may draw this trial balance by seeing that in the life of the entity itself, that which this thought, this study, this reasoning, this introspection, this delving into the inmost conditions, as it were, with this analytical mind of the entity, that which may be set as gain and as loss, and much will be found the gain, even more than there has been in dollars and cents in the ledger, see . . . ?

(Q) Explain what is called "Memory" in terms of subconscious or spiritual development.

(A) As has been given, as is seen, *Memory* becomes the thought, and thought becomes memory—that is, as the various experience of an *entity* (this in the term of the spiritual, of the physical, of the soul entity, see? not as a physical entity meaning of body and mind and physical being, but of the soul entity, the spiritual entity, which is comprised of the subconscious, the spiritual entity, and the superconscious mind), as is seen, see? as of *this* entity, gains the various experiences; for only through experiences does the *building* come in *mind*, see? for, as is seen, by comparison does the building take place—that is, as memory is thought, *Thought* is *Memory*, and *building* one upon the other. This is spiritual thought, spiritual memory.

Reading 1472-3

For, as then, the evolution of man's experiences is for the individual purpose of becoming more and more acquainted with those activities in the relationships with the fellow man, as an exemplification, as a manifestation of Divine Love—as was shown by the Son of man, Jesus; that *each* and every soul *must become, must be*, the *savior* of some soul! to even *comprehend* the purpose of the entrance of the Son *into* the earth— that man might have the closer walk with, yea the open door to, the very heart of the living God!

Reading 1602-5

HLC: You will have before you the entity, [1602], also her mental and material affairs. It has been indicated, thru various sources, that the period immediately ahead, is one of change in many fields—politically, economically, and geologically. Will you clarify these predictions for me, and give directions for me at this time? answering questions which have been prepared?

EC: Yes, we have the entity here.

As in relationship to changes—these are indicated not only through prophecies but through astrological aspects, as well as the thought and intent of persons and groups in high places; bringing about these things, these conditions, in what might be said to be the fullness of time.

However—since the advent of the Son of Man in the earth, giving man an advocate with the Father, there has been an influence that may counteract much of that which has been indicated that would come as retribution, or in filling the law of an evolution of ideas and the relationship of material things to the thoughts and intents of individuals and groups.

Then, as to whether the hearts and minds of individuals or souls (who were given authority concerning the laws of the universe) are fired with the thoughts of dire consequences or those things that bespeak of the greater development of a spiritual awakening, is still in the keeping and in the activities of individuals who—as this entity—have caught a glimpse, or an awareness, of that which is in the making, in the affairs of state, nation, and nations, and the universe, as related to the conditions upon the face of Mother Earth.

There enters much, then, that might become questions as respecting that which has been foretold, or prophesied, as well as respecting the activities of groups and individuals who have acted and who are to act as a counterbalance to these happenings in the earth.

In the first premise—know what was the cause of indifference, or sin, entering material manifestations. Was it the purpose by God that such should be, or by the Godhead? or was it that this force or power seeking expression found—with the expression—that there came the forces of positive and negative?

And with same the awareness of one influence or force, taking certain courses or directions, became negative.

The others became the greater positive.

Reading 254–109

HLC: You will have before you the work of the Association in preparing and presenting a pamphlet on information given through this channel, in life readings and general readings, pertaining to the Essenes' preparation for the coming of Jesus. The writing of this pamphlet is in the hands of Enid S. Smith of 503 West 121st Street, New York, City. You will answer the questions, as I ask them:

EC: Yes, we have the work, the policies and the purposes of the Association for Research and Enlightenment, Incorporated, together with information which has been supplied through this channel—Edgar Cayce; also the work as done on same by Enid S. Smith.

As we find, in the main this has been very well done. There may be made one suggestion as to attempting to make that presented through these sources conform to that which is already a part of the public record.

Draw a parallel, rather than attempting to so word or phrase such paragraphs as to conform. One would be rather the introduction to the other.

Ready for questions.

(Q) Comment fully on just what the purpose, objectives and general tone of this pamphlet should be.

(A) This should be the tone: It is generally conceded by those who are students—in the Christian faith as well as in many other phases of spiritual evolution—that there is the expectancy of a new order, or a fulfilling of or a return to those activities that may bring about the time for that redemption of the world; in a return or in an acknowledgement of that as the basis of the individual instruction or direction. Then, this pamphlet or paper should give to others an insight as to what and how there was the physical, mental and spiritual attitude of that group; as to how those individuals so well acted their part, and yet not becoming known in that presented. So, this may enable individuals and groups to so prepare themselves as to be channels through which the more perfect way may be seen.

(Q) What is the correct meaning of the term "Essene"?

(A) Expectancy.

(Q) Was the main purpose of the Essenes to raise up people who would be fit channels for the birth of the Messiah who later would be sent out into the world to represent their Brotherhood?

(A) The individual preparation was the first purpose. The being sent out into the world was secondary. Only a very few held to the idea of the realization in organization, other than that which would come with the Messiah's pronouncements.

(Q) Were the Essenes called at various times and places Nazarites, School of the Prophets, Hasidees, Therapeutae, Nazarenes, and were they a branch of the Great White Brotherhood, starting in Egypt and taking as members Gentiles and Jews alike?

(A) In general, yes. Specifically, not altogether. They were known at times as some of these; or the Nazarites were a branch or a *thought* of same, see? Just as in the present one would say that any denomination by name is a branch of the Christian-Protestant faith, see? So were those of the various groups, though their purpose was of the first foundations of the prophets as established, or as understood from the school of prophets, by Elijah; and propagated and studied through the things begun by Samuel. The movement was *not* an Egyptian one, though *adopted* by those in another period—or an earlier period—and made a part of the whole movement. They took Jews and Gentiles alike as members—yes.

Reading 5758-1 (Entire reading)

GC: Now you will have before you the Spiritual Life Group of the Park Place Methodist Church, some of whose members are present in this room, while other members are at their homes. You will give at this time advice and counsel regarding their work, and how they may best express the spirit of Christ in their work; and you will answer questions asked concerning any phase of it:

EC: Yes, we have the group—Spiritual Life Group, Park Place Methodist Church—as a group, as individuals.

In analyzing or giving that which may be helpful for this group, many personalities are to be taken into consideration. This should be the ideal of each member of such a group; that the personality of the Christ-Consciousness may be the individuality of each group; also each individual in the group. And as there is the analyzing of the Christ-Life, Christ-Consciousness, one realizes and finds that the Christ-Child was born into the earth as man; one born in due season, in due time, in man's spiritual evolution, that man might have a pattern of the personality and the individuality of God Himself.

Thus as the individuals in such a group read, analyze, study and apply those tenets, those truths that were presented by the Christ, they find that the Christ-Consciousness must become an individual and yet a living thing within their own individual consciousnesses. As with Him, He found no fault in others. This should be the first premise, then, of each individual; less and less condemning of others and more and more of self manifesting that love shown by the Father through the Son in the material world; that man, through this pattern, through this picture of God, may become a living example, may walk closer in that way of less condemning.

For as each individual realizes, as these tenets may be analyzed, if

God had condemned—what opportunity would there be for man to find his way back to God? Thus each individual must do unto others as he would have his Brother, the Christ, his God, the Father, do unto him; and indeed, then, apply first, last and always His "Forgive, O God, as I forgive others. Find fault in me, O God, as I find fault in my brother." Less and less then of self, more and more of perfect love, without dissimulations, keeping that faith. Know that as there is the activity of self, self can only sow the seed of truth. And it will be to each individual as was indicated to the children of Israel. They entered into the Promised Land not because of their righteousness but because of the love of the Father for those who tried, who *tried* to live the righteousness.

Thus each individual may have the try counted as righteousness; not as an excuse, neither as justification. For ye have been justified once for all, through the Christ-Consciousness that ye seek.

Then the life, the purpose of the individual, the members of such a Life Group, should be that they may walk closer to the Christ day by day in every way. For His promise has been and is ever to each soul, "If ye will open thy mind, thy heart, I will enter, I will abide with thee." Not as a stranger, but as a brother, as a friend.

In this manner may the group as a group become a power for good, a power magnifying and glorifying the Christ-Life in the church, in the community, in the nation, in the world. For in this showing of the seed of the spirit ye sow, and God alone may give the increase, God alone may prepare the heart. For eternal life is never earned—it is the gift of God, by the grace of God—through the giving of the life of the Master, Jesus, who became the Christ by overcoming death, hell and the grave, overcoming the world.

Remember as He has given, it must indeed be that offenses come, but woe unto him by whom they come.

Let it never be said, then, of a single member of the group that ye offended the least of any of His little ones.

Think not more highly of thyself than ye ought, nor consider thyself above thy fellow man. For He that is the greatest will be the servant of all. Even as the Master signified in the bathing of the feet, in the breaking of the bread, in the building of the fire, in the preparation of the food; that the weary in body, in mind might be supplied. And then as He gave to that Disciple, He requires of everyone, "feed my lambs, feed my sheep." For all have fallen short, yet recognizing in self that of thyself ye can do nothing, but only as the spirit of truth directeth, ye may accomplish much. Then, entertain only the spirit of truth, the purpose of love, the hope of life. For He gave, "I came that ye might have light, life and love, and have all more abundantly."

And when these things are manifested in the mind and the hearts of the individuals of such a group, yea the world will feel the vibrations, yea the glory of the coming of the Lord. For He tarries not—for some, and in His love abide thee always.

Ready for questions.

(Q) As I give the name of each individual member of the group, will you please give an individual message: [3466].

(A) Let that mind be within thee as was in the Christ, that gave Himself that others might know God. Do thou likewise.

(Q) R. S.

(A) Let grace keep thee. Let mercy and justice direct thee, that the peace which passeth all understanding may be thine in the consciousness of the Christ-Presence.

(Q) [993].

(A) Let love be without dissimulation. Abhor that which is evil. Cleave to that which is good. Try ye the purposes in each, but know that the Lord liveth and seeks the love, the help of others.

(Q) Edna Hainsworth.

(A) Keep thy heart singing. Be not disturbed, nor let fear come in. For perfect love casteth out fear. Keep thy faith in thy Lord, thy Master.

(Q) Hattie Trigg.

(A) Come! Make a joyful noise unto the Lord, Who is thy salvation. Come! Keep thy promises as ye hope that He will keep His promises to thee. Let not doubt nor fear enter, but trust in the Lord.

(Q) [2990].

(A) Of him that hath much, much is required. Be not overzealous nor yet overanxious. For the Lord is in His Holy Temple. Prepare that Temple in thine own body, mind and heart, that He may dwell there—ever.

(Q) [3377].

(A) Keep the way of the Christ ever before thee in thy uprisings, in thy downsettings. For the Lord hath need of thee today in the hearts of many who look to thee for direction. Let thy life, thy conversations, ever point the way to Christ.

(Q) [3374].

(A) Grace and love are virtues in thee. Keep them in suchways and manners that thy life may direct others, though ye speak never a word. For what the body-mind is speaks louder than what people say. Keep the faith.

(Q) [3416].

(A) In the Lord's house are many mansions. In thy mind and heart are many possibilities, many opportunities. Lose not a single one to make known the love that the Master has for the children of men. For He, too, was one of them. So in thy ways of grace and mercy, show forth the Lord's death, the Lord's life, the Lord's love, until He comes again.

(Q) May we have a Christmas message from the Master at this time?

(A) Let not your hearts be troubled, neither let them be afraid. For the Lord is in the Holy Temple—let the earth and those that love the Lord rejoice, that the Father-God in the Christ is mindful of men, and He will not let thy loved ones—nor those with and for whom ye pray—be tempted beyond that they are able to bear. But live daily as ye pray, and pray as ye would have thy brother, the Christ, to praise thy life before the throne of mercy. Show ye mercy and love one to another, then, if ye would have love and mercy shown to thee. For this is the beginning and the end of wisdom.

We are through.

Reading 5246-1

The entity has trained its consciousness to consider others and yet innately there are those rebellions at some of the associations, as we shall see. Thus the entity needs to analyze self; begin at this: Know there is the physical body and its attributes, its hopes, its desires, physical just as that of animated matter, animated spirit.

Then there is the mind, the physical mind and its associations; the spiritual mind and its hopes and desires.

Then there is the soul body also. Thus as you find in self body, mind, soul, in its three-dimensional manner it is as the spiritual three-dimensional concept of the Godhead; Father, Son, Holy Spirit.

These, then, in self are a shadow of the spirit of the Creative Force. Thus as the Father is as the body, the mind is as the Son, the Soul is as the Holy Spirit. For it is eternal. It has ever been and ever will be, and it is the soul made in the image of the Creator, not merely the physical or mental being but with the attributes. For, as is given in the beginning: God moved and said, "Let there be light," and there was light, not the light of the sun, but rather that of which, through which, in which every soul had, has, and ever has its being. For in truth ye live and love and have thy being in Him.

These considerations, then, each in analyzing of self, each has its part in thine own physical consciousness, yes.

Take time to be holy, but take time to play also. Take time to rest, time to recuperate; for thy Master, even in the pattern in the earth, took time to rest, took time to be apart from others, took time to meditate and pray, took time to attend a wedding, to give time to attend a funeral; took time to attend those awakenings from death and took time to minister to all.

So in learning thy experience in the earth, not as routine but at regular periods have thy rest, have thy labors, do feed the mind; do feed the soul just as it is necessary to feed the physical man and these will declare just as much dividend as does that necessity of feeding the body. Without that to be masticated, and without its mastication, it is indigestion and suffering. So with the food for the mind and the soul, it must be masticated and put to use, and these will bring much more harmonious experience.

For ye need those companionships that are in accord with thine own ideas and ye will find them if ye seek. For as has been given: "Behold I stand at the door and knock, if ye will open I will enter." This is not merely a saying, for thy mind seeks a Savior, but most of all companionship of the Master draws that which will bring succor and understanding, peace and harmony. For ye remember, as has been given: 'Do know that offenses come, but woe unto him by whom they come. Ye believe an God, believe also in me. For I have overcome the world." And in Him may ye overcome the world.

Reading 900–17

(Q) It has also been given in these readings that Jesus lived a man and died a man. It has also been given that God so loved the world as to give His only begotten Son to act as an example, in the flesh, to man.

Explain these things to us. How may we regard the truth regarding Jesus in relation to the Jewish and Christian religions, and to all the other religions of the world?

(A) In that the man, Jesus, became the ensample of the flesh, manifest in the world, and the will one with the Father, he became the first to manifest same in the material world. Thus, from man's viewpoint, becoming the only, the first, the begotten of the Father, and the ensample to the world, whether Jew, Gentile, or of any other religious forces. In this we find the true advocate with the Father, in that He, as man, manifest in the flesh the ability of the flesh to make fleshly desires one with the will of the spirit. For God is spirit, and they who worship Him must worship in spirit and in truth, just as Jesus manifested in the flesh, and able to partake of the divine, for making all laws susceptible to the mandates. For the will was one with the Father, and in this we find He takes on all law, and a law unto Himself. For with the compliance, of even an earthly or material law, such an person *is* the law. And in that Jesus lived as man, and died as man, and in that became the ensample to all who *would* approach the Throne of God. As we see in all the religions of the world, we find all approaching those conditions where man may become as the law in his connection with the divine, the supreme, the oneness, of the world's manifestation. In Jesus we find the answer.

(Q) It has been given that the soul is the spiritual force that animates or gives life to the body. What is spirit? What is spiritual force? Is it corporeal or incorporeal? Where may we find the soul force in the body—in the brain, nerve centers or where?

(A) There is a vast deal of difference between spiritual and soul forces, for, as given, each force there has been set guards or bounds. Spirit forces are the animation of *all life* giving life-producing forces in animate or inanimate forces. Spiritual elements become corporeal when we speak of the spiritual body in a spiritual entity; then composed of spirit, soul and the superconsciousness. In the soul forces, and its dwelling in man, we find the animation, the spiritual element, the soul that developing element, and contained in the brain, in the nerve, in the centers of the whole system. As to the specific centers, nearer those centers of the sensory system, physically speaking. In the conditions, then, we find when soul and spirit take flight from the animate forces of an human, we find the deadening of all the centers of the sensory system, with the vitality of the solar plexus system, with the gland of the medulla oblongata, these then controlling the forces, and the life becomes extinct, with soul and spirit, with the super-conscious forces, gone. Then, we have as this: Spiritual element, the vitality, produces the motive forces of the entity, whether physical or spiritual. Spiritual forces being the life, the reproductive principle; the soul the development principle. As we have manifested, or illustrated, in the physical body in nerve tissue: There becomes that principle of the nerve action and the nerve in action. That is, with the expression of some condition bringing distress in the body, the active principle is the spirit. The nerve is the soul, for development.

(Q) What happens to the conscious mind forces and physical forces at death?

(A) The conscious mind forces either are in the soul's development, and in the superconsciousness, or left with that portion of material forces which goes to the reclaiming, or remoulding, of physical bodies, for indwelling of spiritual entities.

(Q) Explain universal forces. Are they forces—

(A) (Mr. Cayce, breaking in:) In this, we find that great indwelling of that force as is given in the bounds about all development, whether mental, soul, or spiritual conditions; the universal being that element through which all becomes manifest in a material world, or a spiritual world. As would be illustrated in the prism separating the elements of light, and showing the active principle of given light or heat in its action, by deflection from the given law, the universal forces are as such. These, we see, become manifest in the material world as the mentality of man develops and gains the knowledge of the laws of the universe, and as man in his mentality gains the knowledge of that law, the deflections become the manifestations of universal laws, and force, manifested through the material world. All such laws, as man develops, will come to the use and benefit of man, there being many illustrations in the present age. The greater we find in the life of Jesus, who only used the universal law, and in the deflection of same, through the life lived, made same manifest in the world, in the last overcoming even the disintegration of the spirit and soul from the physical or corporeal body, and able to force all law to become subjugated to the body, or, as we see, manifest in the electrical forces as used by man. This becoming only an atom in motion, and as the atomic force gathers this, producing such vibration as to create heat, light, and of the various natures, by the kind, class or nature of resistance met in its passage in the cycle given, reducing, or raising the velocity, or better by the class of atomic force it vibrates, either with or against. These are ensamples of portions of universal forces.

Reading 262-119

Just so have we seen and comprehended how that there is the Father, the Son, the Holy Spirit. The Spirit is the movement; as when God the First Cause—called into being *Light* as a manifestation of the influences that would, through their movement (light movement) upon forces yet unseen, bring into being what we know as the universe—or matter; in all its forms, phases, manifestations.

As it has been indicated and given of old, no man hath seen God at any time. Yet they who have seen and who now may experience the consciousness of the Christ-Presence, as manifested in flesh in Jesus, have known *of* God, have seen the figure of Him in what the Christ purposed to do, in the desire with which He acted with and upon those influences and forces of the earth.

And as He gave or taught, we become aware of same through dwelling upon mentally and through applying physically those things we know that partake of that which brings the awareness.

Yet we know, or find, that the kingdom of heaven is within; and that the awareness, the awakening comes from within.

Then through faith, through the gift of the Son and the faith in Him, we become more and more aware of the abiding presence of the spirit—the movement—as prompted by the Father; and not of self.

Ready for questions.

(Q) Please comment on the treatment of the outline, Page 3, "From Whence We Came, How and Why."

(A) This has been commented upon heretofore. As has been indicated, the purpose of the spirit entering into what we know as matter is a different condition or phase of condition from the purpose of entering into spirit as He is Spirit. As those influences or forces entered that took man away *from* Him, then it was from that consciousness or spirit that the individuality had its source, its essence, its influence that might be made a personality in its activity. Hence the entrance into matter became as the description has been given by Stephen, by Philip, by Jesus. "Know ye not that the Son must go up to Jerusalem, there be tried, condemned, and die—even the death on the cross?" *Why?* That there might be indeed an advocate, a *way* to the Father—from the lowest depths of man's desire, man's loathsomeness, even in matter. For if God has not willed that any should perish but has with every temptation prepared a way to meet it, *who* then—*what*, then—is the way? The experiences through which man passes, as God gave in other periods, to become aware of his purpose for entrance into what we know as materiality. Then, the awareness of the *way* comes through the *thought* of man, the *faith* of man, the *desire* of man such as ever held by that One who became *righteousness itself*; passing through all the phases of man's desire in materiality. Then, what meaneth faith—what meaneth hope—what meaneth these things in man's experience. There must be the arousing of that desire for same. Hence how has He put it again? "Indeed it must be that offences come, but woe unto him by whom they come." Not that man is awakened all at once, but here a little, there a little, line upon line, precept upon precept. Then as these are applied, as these become a part of the experience of the soul, there becomes the desire of the soul to find its rest, its peace, its hope in Him who is the Author of faith, of hope, of mercy, of love. Thus does the awareness come as to the purposes of man's advent into what we know as materiality. Thus do we see and comprehend why it was necessary that He, the Son, the Maker, the Creator, come unto His own; who in their blindness, selfishness, hates, spites, have brought and do bring about those influences that keep the heart of man from seeking the Way. But He being the Way, offers—whosoever will, let him come and take of the water of life freely. What is meant then by "the Spirit and the Lamb say come"? or "the Spirit and the Bride saith come"? It means that whosoever will may take hold upon those things that take man's mind and heart and purpose and *being* away from those things that have made men afraid, that have brought all of these petty conditions, spites, heartaches and disappointments. Hark ye, when ye are disappointed, when ye are confused, and think for a moment what it must have been for the Son, for Him who had made the earth and who had been given all power therein, to have His own to receive or understand Him not; yea, those of His own household—yea, those who had come through the channel even as He. Is it any wonder that He said (and do ye comprehend?), "Who is my mother, who is my brother, my sister? He that doeth the will of the father, the same is my mother, my brother, my sister"? These words ye know, but have ye comprehended, have ye understood? For when there has come the slight here, the harsh word there, or the disappointment, have ye smiled and with a song upon thy heart said, "Thy will, O God, not mine, be done"? Until ye do, ye cannot comprehend the purpose for which the souls of men came into materiality; for periods of lessons, of examinations. Know that to be absent from the body is to be present with thy conscience, thy god. What is thy god? Is it self or Christ? Is it self or the Lord? Is it thy own desires and wishes? Or is it that as He manifested when He gave Himself as the ransom, as the way, that He—too—when ye call—might say, "Come—I will give you rest—my yoke is easy, my burden is light"? Then when ye have the least of earthly burdens do ye doubt that He understands; He who has passed through *so much* in materiality, in the *flesh* and blood even as thee? *He* knows! *He* understands! *He* hears thy call and bids thee *come, drink* of the water of life!

Reading 262–60

(Q) In canonizing the Bible, why was the life of Zan [Zend] left out?

(A) Called in other names. For, much might be given respecting that ye have that ye call the Bible. This has passed through many hands. Many that would turn that which was written into the meanings that would suit their own purposes, as ye yourselves often do. But if ye will get the spirit of that written there ye may find it will lead thee to the gates of heaven. For, it tells of God, of your home, of His dealings with His peoples in many environs, in many lands. Read it to be wise. Study it to understand. *Live* it to know that the Christ walks through same with thee. For, as He gave, in righteousness may ye know those things that have been preserved from the foundations of the worlds in thine own experience. For, these are told there in the manners of those that recorded same in their own environ. What wilt *thou* write today that will be as the words of life to thy brothers in the ages to come? For, He has given, ye have been called—and ye have a work to do.

6

●

Soul Development

Reading 3424-1

For all is born first in spirit, then in mind, then it may become manifested in the material plane. For God moved and the heavens and the earth came into being. God is spirit. Man with his soul, that may be a companion to the Creative Forces, is of that same source. Thus to grow in grace and knowledge, one applies, one has, one uses one's spiritual self. And with what spirit we apply, we grow also in mind and in body.

Reading 2058-1

As may have been indicated from the first premise of the activity of an individual entity or soul in material experience—no entity enters by chance, but as from the will of the Father, through that application of each entity or soul respecting its development or its evolution to its estate for which there is the purpose of expression, namely: to be as a companion with the Creative Forces, or God.

Hence the entrance of each entity into an experience in the material or manifested form is that this desire, this purpose, may be furthered in its evolution or its development towards those relationships which the entity, as a unit, bears towards the Creative Forces, or God-Activity.

Hence the purpose for each soul's entrance is that it may have the greater opportunity under the environs or associations or activities that are necessary for the proving of, or the developing towards, that very purpose or experience in the affairs of each entity.

Thus the growth depends upon how well the adherence in relationships one to another is in that direction of making manifest the glory as seen, or felt, or sought, in Creative Forces.

Hence all purposes, all desires, all growth, depend upon what attitude each takes towards Creative Forces.

The ideas and ideals, then, and the application of self in the material relationships, should be in keeping with that which is ever constructive in the experience, and never of the material or the mercenary nature as the first cause; for, as the intent is manifested, each soul, each entity lives and moves and has its being in the Creative Forces.

Thus there is latent within each soul the ability to make itself one with the Creative Force.

Thus the expression is made manifest that as you do it day by day to those about you, you do to your Maker—or to your better self.

Then, to take advantage, or to create that in the experience of others which brings dissension, disputes and hate, and such, is to bring disturbance, dis-ease, disheartening, disloyalty to self.

For as ye do it unto these, ye do it unto thy Maker.

Reading 5749-3 (Entire reading)

GC: You will give at this time a discourse on the subject, "Angels and Archangels, and How They Help Humanity." You will also answer the questions which will be asked.

EC: Yes. With the bringing into creation the manifested forms, there came that which has been, is, and ever will be, the spirit realm and its attributes—designated as angels and archangels. They are the spiritual manifestations in the spirit world of those attributes that the developing forces accredit to the One Source, that may be seen in material planes through the influences that may aid in development of the mental and spiritual forces through an experience—or in the acquiring of knowledge that may aid in the intercourse one with another.

Then, how do they aid? Under what law do they operate?

The divine, in its intercourse, influence and manifestation with that which partakes of the same forces as they manifest.

Ready for questions.

(Q) Please explain the virgin birth of Jesus, the Christ.

(A) In that there had been the manifestation in the earth of that which completed the cycle for the necessary manifestation in the earth of the holy influence necessary for the sustaining of a backsliding world, there was then that choosing of the influence through which there became manifest (in and through those channels that comply with the laws of spiritual forces) that which brought into being the conception, that made for the living influence of the Spirit through the body that became the child Jesus; and through the manifesting of the spirit of the oneness of the Father became a manifestation of the Christ Spirit in material surroundings.

(Q) Explain the law of the line of demarcation between soul and spirit.

(A) This is one, yet distinct—even as the Father, the Son, the Holy Spirit is one, yet is the manifestation of a force that is capable of manifestation in the varied planes of development. The soul is an individual, individuality, that may grow to be one with, or separate from, the whole. The spirit is the impelling influence of infinity, or the one creative source, force, that is manifest. Hence we find that in the physical plane we seek soul manifestation as the spirit moves same in activity.

(Q) Discuss the various phases of spiritual development before and after reincarnation in the earth.

(A) This may be illustrated best in that which has been sought through example in the earth. When there was in the beginning a man's advent into the plane known as earth, and it became a living soul, amenable to the laws that govern the plane itself as presented, the Son of man entered earth as the first man. Hence the Son of man, the Son of God, the Son of the first Cause, making manifest in a material body. This was not the first spiritual influence, spiritual body, spiritual manifestation in the earth, but the first man—flesh and blood; the first carnal house, the first amenable body to the laws of the plane in its position in the universe. *For, the earth is only an atom in the universe of worlds!* And man's development began through the laws of the generations in the earth; thus the development, retardment, or the alterations in those positions in a material plane. And with error entered that as called *death*, which is only a transition—or through God's other door—into that realm where the entity has builded, in its manifestations as related to the knowledge and activity respecting the law of the universal influence. Hence the development is through the planes of experience that an entity may become one *with* the first cause; even as the angels that wait before the Throne bring the access of the influence in the experience through the desires and activities of an entity, or being, in whatever state, place or plane of development the entity is passing. For, in the comprehension of no time, no space, no beginning, no end, there may be the glimpse of what simple transition or birth into the material is; as passing through the other door into another consciousness. Death in the material plane is passing through the outer door into a consciousness in the material activities that partakes of what the entity, or soul, has done with its spiritual truth in its manifestations in the other sphere. Hence, as there came the development of that first entity of flesh and blood through the earth plane, he became *indeed* the Son—through the things which He experienced in the varied planes, as the development came to the oneness with the position in that which man terms the Triune.

(Q) Are angels and archangels synonymous with that which we call the laws of the universe? If so, explain and give an example.

(A) They are as the laws of the universe; as is Michael the lord of the Way, *not* the Way but the lord of the Way, hence disputed with the influence of evil as to the way of the spirit of the teacher or director in his entrance through the outer door. [See Jude 1:9 in re Michael the archangel "when contending with the devil about the body of Moses" when Moses died.]

(Q) Describe some of the planes into which entities pass on experiencing the change called death.

(A) Passing from the material consciousness to a spiritual or cosmic, or outer consciousness, oft does an entity or being not become conscious of that about it; much in the same manner as an entity born into the material plane only becomes conscious gradually of that designated as time and space for the material or third dimensional plane. In the passage the entity becomes conscious, or the recognition of being in a fourth or higher dimensional plane takes place, much in the same way as the consciousness is gained in the material. For, as we have given, that we see manifested in the material plane is but a shadow of that in the spiritual plane. In materiality we find some advance faster, some grow stronger, some become weaklings. Until there is redemption through the acceptance of the law (or love of God, as manifested through the Channel or the Way), there can be little or no development in a material or spiritual plane. But all must pass under the rod, even as He—who entered into materiality.

We are through.

Reading 505-4

HLC: You will have before you the soul entity now known as [505], present in this room. You will give a mental and spiritual reading for this entity, giving the reason for entrance into this cycle of experience, trace the soul development and guide the entity to its complete expression of the highest soul development in this life. You will answer the questions which may be asked.

EC: Yes, we have the soul-entity here, [505].

In the approaches for the understanding of soul development for this entity's comprehension or understanding, well that this also be given:

In entering an experience in the material plane, the entity or soul sees through what environs it may pass. That man has divided into time and in different periods of an entity's experience in the earth (being divided into expressions of one environ and another) is viewed as a whole or as a unit, from the soul's sojourn in entering. And the soul's manifestation depends upon what the soul-mind may do with the opportunities that may be presented to that body or soul through an experience. As to what, is asked? That which may be to the soul the more worthy expression of that which is creative, or that which is the activity of what has rightly been termed to man as the fruits of the spirit, or truth and light, and the expression of man's relationship to the Creative Forces in the activity. That man in the realm of man's sojourn may only express or manifest same upon or to the associates or those whom the soul or the entity may contact is as an expression that is viewed by all.

Then, in entering, each soul comes to manifest that it has *not* so well learned in the lessons of hope, patience, tolerance, brotherly love, kindness, gentleness, meekness, and such. These are the fruits of the spirit. And the manifestation of these attributes in the experience of each soul brings, as the Master of Masters has given, that awareness of self of the soul that is the gift of the Creator, that is the birthright of every individual that may be wasted in attempting to gratify those things that are of the earth, or of the carnal forces, and thus become weakened and less aware of its experience or existence in the affairs of man. Yet the soul finds its experience, no matter in what environ; and the *environ* is that created by what the soul—the inner self—has done, does do, about the manifestations of Creative Influences in the relationships to its fellow man.

For, as has been given of old, the Father needeth not *any* attribute or any help that man may do. Yet each soul may be a channel, a god, a savior, a friend in the time of need. For, those that would find God must believe that He is, and in the daily walks of life give expressions of that which is an attribute that self would attribute to the Father. And thus may the soul become in patience, in hope, in faith, in love, aware of the Father's indwelling within it.

That each soul has an advocate with the Father through the gift of the Christ into the soul and into the experiences of men is manifested in the experience of most all peoples. That man or men, or peoples, in various channels or activities have misapplied, misused these activities for the gratifying of their own selfish interests—or used the cloak of some name or some activity to hide behind—these are ever present. For, as of old, it is given to each and every soul, "There is today set before you good and evil, life and death—choose thou." As is the choice, as is known in the experience of each soul, as the application is made in the experience, so are the fruits. "By their fruits ye shall know them."

Then, when a choice has been made that makes for those things that bring contention, avarice, vice, harsh words, know there must be a renewing of self in those hopes and promises He has given. And though the choice has been ill, the activities may bring peace and harmony and understanding, and the glorifying ever to the Father through that it causes the individual to do *to* its neighbor, its friend, its associates. For, as He has given, "He that giveth the cup of cold water in the name of the Son shall in no wise lose his reward," in that harmony, peace and life that is expressed in the activities of such a soul.

So, in the experience of this entity, there have come those experiences wherein there has been seen—even in the present experience—avarice, and what (to self) may have been injustice, in unkind words and in harshnesses of activity. Yet, when the trust has been put in Him that

giveth life, there has come from same rather the fruits of the spirit;
that has made for greater peace, harmony, beauty in the expressions
of thought and activity in the experiences of others.

So, in thine development, let those words be the echo of all that thou
wouldst do, that in the name of the Father—through the love as shown
in the Son—the life may be guided day by day in its walks before men;
and thus may there come to this soul the harmonious influences that
make for the life being more worth while in the expressions of same, as
it goes about meeting the daily activities that come in the expressions
of self, bringing glory, honor in thine self through the love the Father
has shown in the sons of men.

For, as He has given, the new commandment comes unto every soul,
"that ye love one another even as the Father hath loved you;" and love
overcometh, love looketh not upon these things that are unlovely, it
vaunteth not itself, it speaketh no evil, and begets love and friendship
in *every* way and manner.

Thus in the expression of self in this experience to learn more of
what love means in the manifestations of the acts of individuals *towards*
its fellow man.

Ready for questions.

(Q) Are there any important directions for my physical condition that
will aid in my whole development?

(A) As has been pointed out, there are the necessities of keeping an
even balance throughout the whole of the physical body, that each
portion—each in its own sphere of activity—will coordinate and coop-
erate with the rest of the system, that the greater balance may be kept.
That there have been warrings within, as has been demonstrated by
the conditions that have existed in the physical forces, is apparent. But
if these are kept in accord, through bringing into the experience as has
been outlined for the body—the necessary elements and the necessary
activities physical and mental, there will be created for the body that
which it has need of, for its own best physical and mental development.

(Q) What work has God planned for me in this life?

(A) Rather would it be said, what have I thus far in my earthly experiences fitted myself to do that I may in the present give the better
expression of God's love in the earth, thus using the mind, the soul, the
body, for greater expression of God in the earth and for the greater soul

development of self? It is imminent, and apparent, that the abilities lie in the fields of activity that portray to others the beauties seen in the earth. And in these expressions, and in aiding others to find the expressions for themselves of that which may make in their experience the greater development of themselves, will be and is the work for which self has been fitted. For, as has been given, when the entity, the soul, came into the earth to find an expression, and to give expression in the experience of others that love might rule in the earth in its every phase of activity in the ways of manifesting same, the expressing of that beauty becomes a portion of the work of the hands—as in art, in those directions that give expressions of nature and its activity in the earth—and in the lives of others that the entity may meet, not only in tolerance but also in love, that they—too—as individuals may find their expressions in the earth in ways and means to, through their own activity, glorify the Father that giveth the increase in peace and harmony and beauty and glory forever.

Reading 69–3

(Q) Please explain cause of seeming standstill of spiritual progress?

(A) The *physical* condition!

(Q) How may I gain a greater understanding in my evolution than otherwise I am doing?

(A) Do not be weary in well-doing. Keep that thou hast. Follow in that thou knowest, and—as given—it is step by step. Do not be impatient.

(Q) Did I come here to do a specific work?

(A) As *all* have a specific work, so are the activities of self to be in cleansing self's own understanding and enabling others to find the way to know themselves and Him.

(Q) Have I been the means of helping many through meditation?

(A) Many, many, many.

(Q) Do I go about it in the right way?

(A) As the results have come, and as the conditions are changed for self, then the changes as to the manner or way may be changed. As results or fruits are shown, keep in the way that has been given.

(Q) Is it necessary for one to feel vibration in helping others?

(A) Not necessary, unless there is felt within self that it must be a form of expression. If the results come, then it is known. How often gave He that "Virtue has gone out of me," or that the vibration by the touch of faith had required strength of Him? for, as it has been given, each in their *own* way and manner approach that *necessary* for the accomplishing of the *knowing* of wherein the help cometh. Find not fault with another, that their own approach is different. Only aid in that thou knowest.

Reading 585-12

Use all such in constructive, creative forces and we will find it will enable the entity to become more and more at peace with itself, more and more able to control the emotions of the body itself; becoming less and less subject to the needs or the usage of material things. For, when a soul becomes so encumbered with the material things, the mental and spiritual are relegated to the background too often. Or, as was expressed by Him, "How hard indeed for a rich man to enter the kingdom of heaven." Yet the kingdom of heaven is within, and the desire for material things—as the desire for pleasures of material things—relegates the spiritual purpose and desires too oft to secondary place in the experience of souls. Do not let this become a part of thine own experience. Because of the equalization of temptations these may become easier, but forget not His ways; and keep the purposes and the faith and the hope and the patience, first and foremost.

Reading 275-39

EC: Yes, we have the entity here, now known as [275].

In entering the present experience for its own soul development, as has been indicated, there were many factors that determined the present entrance, and with many of those conditions that were in that realm of meeting influences that had been expressed in activities in sojourns of the entity in the earth's experience. Yet the purposes, the desires, were for self–expression under the influence and guidance of that which had influenced activity in relationships to self and others in soul and mental development of the entity.

As has oft been given through these channels, and as may be well illustrated in that which has been given respecting the development of this entity, what one soul does about the knowledge and understanding that the soul has *of* the Creative Forces in its experience makes for the developments or the retardments, or builds in the experience that which must of necessity be met in an activity as related to individuals and to self. Self-expression, self-development, then, is the desire, purpose, aim of the soul in its manifestations in the earth in the present experience.

As to how there may be the development of the mental and psychic forces of the entity, well that there be some comprehension of mental and soul development. Soul is that which is the gift of the Creator to be the individuality that must present itself before the Throne for judgment in its experiences through activities in whatsoever realm it, the soul, may find itself. Mind is that active force that makes for the awareness or consciousness of the activity being in this, that or the other realm. Hence it partakes of a physical condition, of a purely mental condition, and of the soul or the spirit condition, and has in the minds of many been divided and given names that have not altogether set the metes and bounds about same; hence cause confusion oft in the experience of others—or those who find activities in the various spheres and are accredited to that as may be set rather into metes and bounds, rather than considering that soul and spirit *has* no bounds save that it, the soul, has builded or made for itself in respects to that it has had the association or connection with as respecting its activity in building to or from its Creative Force in its experience.

Hence we find, as has been indicated in this entity's and soul's experience, that which illustrates, demonstrates, that as has oft been given respecting what individuals or souls have done respecting that they knew within themselves to be that which was creative and that which was selfish.

That which is so hard to be understood in the minds or the experiences of many is that the activities of a soul are for self-development, yet must be selfless in its activity for it, the soul, to develop.

Take for the moment that which may be illustrated in a physical body, as may be illustrated in this body—as to where conditions are to take place, are taking place, that may very well illustrate that point here that we would make for the entity, and for those that would study respecting self and self's development, yet being selfless in their development.

As has been given by Him as the teacher, as the minister, as the savior to all men, "I of myself can do nothing. The Father that worketh *in* me, *he* doeth the works that you see." When the body is using of itself that which is the Creative Force in itself, we see—as in this body—it uses its very own self; hence is selfishness, or the aggrandizing of the qualities in the mental forces of the body–physical or in the mental intelligentsia of the body itself, and has forgotten or neglects that which is creative or constructive in itself. Yet when the body–physical and mental and spiritual uses itself in giving to another that which is helpful, hopeful *to* that soul, it draws from that source in the spiritual influences, or God, to give to the other. Hence the illustration that has been thus drawn.

In the development then of the soul forces of this entity, [275], called in the present, as has been given, the title, the name, is written; that is, there is the desire, there is the wish, there is the longing to be used by self, to use self, to be used by the Creative Forces in giving to others that which will in themselves arouse the understanding and the knowledge of the indwelling of the spiritual life within self that may quicken the soul to its own duties, opportunities, abilities, as related to *their* influences and *their* relationships with the Creative Forces. Hence is the title, is the name written within self, and recorded with those that have given His angels charge concerning thine activities, that there be no stumbling within the experience of this soul.

Then, to awaken that within self that may be the more helpful, that will make self the greater channel for others, that will bring into the physical forces of the body–physical that which will renew, regenerate those forces from within, that the applications that may be made without may become one in their activity to the glorification of the Father, there needs be only that the trust remain in Him and that there be the arousing to those consciousnesses of His presence dwelling in thine own experience and in thine own heart and soul, that every atom, every cell within the whole physical body, mind and soul becomes attuned to those spheres of activity that are aroused by the consciousness of His presence being with thee. For, there are the abilities to give out to others. Enter, then, into the closet of thine own heart, purging same with the hyssop, with the blood of the Father through the Christ. In so doing may the consecration of the purposes and desires of the heart become one with Him. Then, as that given is poured out or given to the other, there may come in thine experience the oneness of *his* purposes with thine own, and thus may the soul become aware in the patience; as He has given that we become aware of the souls in same. Know that He liveth in thee, in the acts of thine mind, of thine body, and thus may ye gather around the Throne of mercy and grace and peace and light, and with the angels give glory to the Lamb of God that taketh away the sins and the errors of those that trust in Him. And thus may the physical consciousness become aware that there is the Lamb that joins with thee in making intercession for those that need his redeeming grace and love; making aware in that given thee in thy activities, that others may know that the seal is set in the Christ, the Lamb of God.

Ready for questions.

(Q) Outline a method of meditation which will help me the most in my psychic development, giving best time, and prayer.

(A) As has been indicated, in that manner as seemeth to thine own conscience purge thine body with pure water and with those influences whether in tones of color, of music, or of odors, as the conscience, as the desire of the heart is, so surround self—and with that blessing as He gave, that "May His peace and His blessings surround you as ye enter into that oneness with Him in the inner chamber." And with such a meditation or prayer as: *I am thine, O Lord. Use me now as thou seest fit that I, even in my weakness, may claim thy strength in and through me. Purge me as thou seest I have need of, that I may be the better channel for the manifesting of the love of the father through the Christ at this time.*

Reading 281-24

The law, then, is compliance with the universal spiritual influence that awakens any atomic center to the necessity of its concurrent activity in relationships to other pathological forces or influences within a given body. Whether this is by spiritual forces, by any of the mechanical forces, it is of necessity one and the same. Many are the divisions or characters of those ills that befall or become a portion of each individual body. Some are set in motion so that certain portions of the glandular system or of the organs of the body perform more than their share. Hence some are thin, some are fat, some are tall, some are short.

What said He? Can anyone by taking thought make one hair white or black, or add one cubit to his stature? *Who* giveth healing, then?

It is in any manner the result only of compliance to the First Cause, and the activity of same within the individual's *relative* relation to its own evolution.

Ready for questions.

(Q) Is group action more effective than individual, and if so why?

(A) "Where two or three are gathered in my name, I am in the midst of them." These words were spoken by Life, Light, Immortality, and are based on a law. For, in union is strength. Why? Because as there is oneness of purpose, oneness of desire, it becomes motivative within the active forces or influences of a body. The multiplicity of ideas may make confusion, but added cords of strength in one become of the nature as to increase the *ability* and influence in every expression of such a law.

Reading 900-16 (Entire reading)

GC: You will have before you the reading on [900], with questions on subject matter, given December 31st, 1924, at 1:10 P.M. [900-15], and you will continue with the answers to the questions, as I ask them.

EC: Yes, we have the body, the mental forces, the enquiring mind, the seeking for knowledge with the entity, [900], and the subject matter as given.

We would study well that as has been given, and apply self in this present earth plane, that the gifts as are accorded the entity may manifest in this present day and generation. Be not as him who was given one talent and hid same for fear of the austere giver, but rather as him who was given ten talents, that more may be added unto him, until he enter into that as was given, "Enter into the joys of thy labors, and sit down on the right hand, for as thou hast been faithful over a few, I will make thee ruler over many." Enter into the work, then, with an humble heart, and with the joy of the labor, and the peace and the blessings of many will come to thee.

Ready for questions.

(Q) Explain the various planes of eternity, in their order of development, or rather explain to us the steps through which the soul must pass to climb back into the arms of beloved God.

(A) These, we see, must be manifest only as the finite mind in the flesh. As in the spirit forces, the development comes through the many changes, as made manifest in the evolution of man. In the development in eternity's realm, is that a finite force as made of creation may become one with the Creator, as a unit, atom, or vibration, becomes one with the universal forces. When separated, as each were in the beginning, with the many changes possible in the material forces, the development then comes, that each spirit entity, each earth entity, the counterpart of the spirit entity, may become one with the Creator, even as the ensample to man's development through flesh, made perfect in every manner; though taking on flesh, yet without spot or blemish, never condemning, never finding fault, never bringing accusation against any, making the will one with the Father, as was in the beginning. For, without passing through each and every stage of development, there is not the correct vibration to become one with the Creator, beginning with the first vibration, as is of the spirit quickened with the flesh, and made manifest in material world (earth's plane). Then, in the many stages of development, throughout the universal, or in the great system of the universal forces, and each stage of development made manifest through flesh, which is the testing portion of the universal vibration. In this manner then, and for this reason, all made manifest in flesh, and development, through the eons of time, space, and *called* eternity.

(Q) What is this spirit entity in the body, [900], and how may he develop it in the right direction?

(A) This is only the portion that develops other than in the earth's plane. Spirit entity. For soul's development is in the earth's plane. The spirit entity is in the spirit plane.

(Q) Does the spirit entity have a separate consciousness apart from the physical, and is it as the consciousness of [900] when he dreams, or has visions, while asleep?

(A) The spirit entity is a thing apart from any earthly connection in sleep, yet connected. For the earthly or material consciousness is ever tempered with material conditions; the superconsciousness with the consciousness between soul and spirit, and partakes of the spiritual forces principally. In consciousness we find only projections of subconscious and superconscious, which conditions project themselves in dreams, visions, unless entered into the superconscious forces. In the consciousness of earthly or material forces there enters all the attributes of the physical, fleshly body. In the subconscious there enters the attributes of soul forces, and of the conscious forces. In the superconscious there enters the subconscious forces, and spiritual discernment and development.

(Q) Does the spiritual entity, after leaving this earth's plane, have full realization of the physical life, or experience through which it passed while on earth's plane?

(A) It may, should it so choose. As has been given. As in this: In the way that the spiritual insight was given into the heart and soul of Saul of Tarsus, as he beheld his Master in that realm to which he had passed. The consciousness in the material world, through the material consciousness of another material individual. The vision as beheld by him, in the way that of the superconscious manifests in his subconsciousness.

(Q) The body, [900], has now full realization of [Mr. Cayce, breaking in: "No, he hasn't the full realization of this, as yet."] his individuality and of the personalities about him, all being in this earth's plane. Will that full realization remain with him in the next plane, or when he leaves this earth's sphere? Will he know he was [900] on earth, an individual with definite personality and character, and will he be able to realize that which he was and that which he has become?

(A) When he, [900], has reached that perfect realization of these consciousnesses of personae and personalities of individuals, and of self, (to which he may develop) he will become able to attain such superconsciousness in a spiritual plane, as has been outlined. At present, no.

(Q) Now give this body, [900], that information which will lead him, when in communion with his God, and when in vision while asleep, to the knowledge of why the soul was fated to enter into all these experiences in order to develop of its own free will to perfection, and then return to God, when God first created souls in a perfect state. Was it to force the spirit to choose with its will the righteous path to God, in spite of any circumstances and conditions? Was it to see if that which once created perfect would return to the perfect? Explain and illustrate?

(A) This we find has been given, and is manifest in the life of the lowly Nazarene. As has been given, man was made a little lower than the angels, yet with that power to become one with God, while the angel remains the angel. In the life, then, of Jesus we find the oneness made manifest through the ability to overcome all of the temptations of the flesh, and the desires of same, through making the *will one with the Father*. For as we find, oft did He give to those about Him those injunctions, "Those who have seen me have seen the Father," and in man, He, the Son of Man, became one with the Father. Man, through the same channel, may reach that perfection, even higher than the angel, though he attend the God.

We are through for the present.

Reading 1158-6

The expressions of a soul-entity are influenced, as we have so oft given, by what an entity has done regarding its ideal in a given experience. For, to be sure, the entity's development in the process of application makes for the varied effects. Hence when individuals or personalities are contacted the same is applicable; and it is rather then conditions than personalities that are to be met in relationships to individuals oft in varied experiences. Not always to be sure—but these should not be confusing; yet to many who hold so much to personality they become so.

Did not John come as the voice of one crying in the wilderness and in the spirit of Elijah? Yet he *was* Elijah. But those very conditions that were as activities in the one experience and in the other experience were not necessarily (though they were in part) met in individualities, or the soul-entity of those that brought disturbances in the experience of the soul-entity in each appearance.

So, with each soul in its personal appearance, it has varied experiences with conditions expressed in entities—or the entities themselves expressing the condition, or both. These become then as manners in which an entity may find the study of its associations, when the book of remembrance is opened for such an entity.

But as the interpretation of that as may be translated from various experiences, remember that same development that is a part of the whole of creation for its evolution is in action. And these shall not be then so oft interpreted for that as may be termed too literal a translation. For, because an individual may have been wed or an individual may have been associated in activities with an individual entity does not signify that they may be in the identical association, but they will be in a *relative* position—if their associations in a given appearance are such as to become more and more active in the experience of an entity.

Else, how would the life of a patriarch—or as a man of God, or a teacher—become an influence, save as a condition? Not as a personality but a condition—that motivates through the mental forces of an individual or an entity in its experiences.

Thus there becomes constantly that choosing of the relationships of the ideals of an entity as to the relationship of the *ideal* to man's or a soul's relationship to Creative Energy.

Reading 1472–12

For, as has so oft been indicated through the promises, the proclamations, the pronouncements of the saints of old (of which the entity might justly be called one), it has ever been given that God hath not willed that any soul should perish, but hath with every temptation prepared a way, a manner of escape.

Thus—not as a boastfulness, but in all humbleness,—it should be realized in the mental and spiritual attributes of the entity, as well as from that gathered from the experiences through its material sojourn, that the entity's activity is a channel, a means whereby God, the Father, hath insured the carrying forward of His purposes. And to thee He hath entrusted the keeping of the way open; that others may take heart, may be encouraged, may be shown a way, a manner.

This then becomes the whole duty of self at this particular period or phase of man's experience in the earth.

When the entity views conditions—of which it is aware, as the world is aware—it realizes that there is the seeking, the search more and more being made for some light, some hope, some *assurance* that God is still mindful of the children of men; that though they may have wandered far afield, though they may come to those crossroads in all phases of their experience, He is ready to answer when they call.

Also individuals are becoming more and more aware that the greater blessings, the greater experiences, the more worth while things in their lives are those not bought with money, nor by patting the other fellow upon the back only; but with love, patience, hope, brotherly love—just being kind one to another!

Then, it is the job of the entity—whatever the circumstance or environ may be—to bring to others whom ye meet day by day, more and more the awareness of that consciousness; that those *are* the fruits of the spirit—and that, those who masticate, those who master them in their own experience, in their relationships to their fellow men day by day, thereby *become* conscious or aware of that love which was and is manifested in the purposes of the Christ-life in the earth, through Jesus of Galilee!

In the early portions of the experiences in the Egyptian land the entity brought helpful forces in the lives of those who went about choosing what manner of bodies would be the greater channels of, or for, the manifestations of spiritual truths, and for the greater mental development, that the spiritual evolution might be manifested in the earth.

So, as the entity applies such in its experience today, it finds that need to adhere not so much to a formula of exercise physically, or to such mental gymnastics as to expand the mental self, but to the living, thinking, *being* just patient, just kind; leaving aside those things that so easily beset, and looking to the *renewing* of a righteous purpose within; and then *so* living, *so* speaking, *so* acting in conversation and in *every* phase of the life.

For instance—the entity may speak to those who open the door of a morning—whether it be to the cage or to the street—in such a manner that the whole day is brighter because of a kindness expressed.

Would that men, then, *everywhere*, would learn such a lesson!

Then, in this era, this age of changes being wrought, it behooves the entity (as everyone), in its relationships in any manner, to impress upon others in every walk of life—not impelling by force, but by love—to *try* God; to listen to the voice within; to open self to the love that is manifested in gentleness and kindness, and not to the lust for power nor to what others may say, but rather keeping in that attitude which He expressed in that period of manifestation when He said, "Others may do as they may, but as for me, I will serve a *living* God," not one far off. Not one who may not be touched by the infirmities of those who are oppressed and cry unto Him; but when ye pray, when ye cry, that prayer, that cry, must be consistent with the life that is lived in relationship to others day by day.

Indeed man through all periods has with one voice blessed God and with the same cursed his brother. This, as the entity understands, should not be! Yet it is such in the world today that is bringing the seeking for might and power.

As to the manners in which the entity applies those influences which it attained or gained through the periods when it again announced to the children of men the great and mighty day of the Lord being at hand—ye are coming to the realization that the fulfilling of that promise in Him is *today*; for He *is* the way, the truth and the light!

It is no longer, then, afar off; but lo, it is within the heart and mind of each soul—*everywhere*!

For, whosoever *will* may take of the cup of life, and drink—in such measures that the thirsting is no more for those things that put fear and dread into the hearts of the children of men.

For it is neither in this temple, that city, nor the other land, but in thine own heart, in thine own mind.

And *this* ye are to proclaim in thy service through the activities in which ye may be engaged, of whatever nature; whether as the assistant in the script for thine own broadcasts, or in that help ye may give to others.

Know, even as He hath given, if ye enter into the closet of thine own consciousness and *there* give that prayer, that longing, *he* will reward thee openly—as He does thy brethren.

And as ye write, in whatever form or manner is chosen, express again and *again* that the day of the Lord is at hand! and that each soul, *everywhere*, partakes of same—in the fruits of the spirit, that are the holy gifts to every soul. For indeed, as He has given, he that gives the cup of water shall not lose his reward, Christ's reward, God's purpose.

So in thy ministering, in thy conversation, in thy daily activities, let these truths be *constantly* impressed upon the minds of those in *every* walk of life!

To the mother, as she cares for her offspring; though the trials of the material things may be heartrending, that smile, that kindly word gives hope to one who may even be burdened with the thought of how and in what manner the provisions of the day may be supplied!

For, know—as ye have found and have seen manifested so oft—to such as minister to those in every walk of life there comes oft those blessings as He hath indicated, see, may not the very windows of heaven be opened and a blessing poured out on such!

Then indeed count thyself as one blessed beyond most, that thou hast been counted worthy to be entrusted with such a message, and given the ability to express same in such beautiful messages—to the mother, to the father, to the children, to the disconsolate, to the brokenhearted, to those in every walk of life! that they, too, may catch a glimpse of the love which God bestoweth upon the children of men!

For indeed, as thou hast experienced throughout thy sojourns in the earth, and as ye find in the present, putting behind the things that so easily beset, ye may press on to the mark of the higher calling that is set in Him.

And as ye give, it increaseth in thy hand, in thy deed, in thy meditation, in thy activity—everywhere.

Then, let thy heart take more hope. Condemn not that ye be not condemned. *Love* that ye may be loved. Show mercy that ye may have mercy shown. Show patience that ye may indeed become aware of thy relationship to Him.

Reading 1565-1

As to those conditions that the entity be warned of in the latter portion of life, these, as are seen, are forewarnings. Then, being forewarned, be forearmed, for the *Will*—as is the gift of the Creator to man, made a little lower than the angels, with the power of choosing for self as to whether the entity that is given in the body will be One with the Creator or attempt to set up self in that position of atvariance with that Creator, as is seen in him who made war in heaven—in this position, then, the entity must build for self. The conditions are set, even as the Lord has given, "This day I have set before thee good and evil. Choose thou whom thy peoples and thy self will serve," for the Lord is not far off, but is in thine own heart, and the manner and way that the application of self, and self's abilities, to those entities, those individuals, about one's self, is that entity's conception, to others, of that creative force. Use, then, that thou hast in thy hands, as the means to correct many conditions as have been builded within thine own self, and make thyself first right with Him and His laws, through the service that *thy self* may render to thy brothers.

Reading 900-19

(Q) Explain the plane of spirit and soul forces, and what relation this plane has to earth. You will start with death, as we know it.

(A) In that moment—as in birth we have the beginning of an earthly sojourn, little or long, as time may be—as the birth into the spiritual plane begins with the death in earth plane; merely the separation of the spiritual and soul forces from the earthly connections.

Reading 262–114 (Entire reading)

GC: You will have before you Group #1, members of which are present here, and its work on the lesson *Spirit*. You will continue the discourse on this lesson and answer the questions.

EC: Yes, we have the group as gathered here—and their work on the lesson *Spirit*.

As has been indicated, this is the beginning, the end of self-development—*if* it is applied in the experience of the individuals.

Then it behooves us that we give an interpretation, an explanation, of what is in reality meant when many of the accepted terms are indicated in the individual expression.

This to be sure is a question then within the realm of the metaphysical as well as in the material.

Then we should be able to answer ever for the cause, the purpose that we have within us, for every question that may arise respecting such.

The spirit of the times! What do we mean?

The spirit of the age! We here speak of the spirit of America, the spirit of '76, the spirit of the pioneer! What do we mean?

We hear again of the spirit of Fascism, the spirit of the Japanese. What do we mean?

The Spirit of God, the Spirit of Christ, the Spirit of the Church, the Spirit of Truth—what do we mean?

It has been given, has it not, that there is *one* Spirit?

Then what is the meaning of this confusion of words?

When we speak of the spirit of the departed, what do we mean? From whence arose such terms?

Again it has been given that we know nothing that we have not experienced in this material world. What is meant?

When the Master spoke to Peter and said—" . . . flesh and blood hath not revealed *it* unto thee, but my Father which is in heaven"—was that an indication that the Spirit is divided? Is the same meant when He said a few minutes later "Get thee behind me, Satan—thou savourest not the things that be of God (the Spirit), but those that be of men (the earth)"?

What is the spirit of the earth? What has He given?

These then must be questions; not only questions but answers. For as they have been asked of us here, they must in truth be answered in such a manner that we—each of us—may make them practical, applicable, practical in our experiences day by day.

Then we must begin, my beloved, at the beginning of how, where, when such things came to be a terminology; or expressed in such manners that there appeared to be, or *appears* to be, or *may* appear to be, a diffusion, a separation; that only those who *have* the desire for the seeking and knowing the truth *may* correctly interpret.

For remember, as has been given by Him, flesh and blood may *not* reveal it unto us—it is the gift of the Father; that we may be lights unto the children of men, to those that sit in darkness, to those that are confused, to those that have made their opportunities stumbling stones rather than stepping-stones.

But these must then answer, ever, in all good conscience, to all that seek to know.

Then the basic or first causes, as Spirit came to materiality, must be sought out. And to be understandable to man, to be comprehended by all, they—the first causes, the answers—must conform to that which has been ever given, in *any* condition, in *any* experience of man in his seeking in this material world. They must answer for that which was, that which is, and that which will be.

Then we must know from whence we came; how, why; and whence we go—and why.

In God's own purpose, Spirit is His presence then. For the Spirit of God moved and that which is in matter came into being, for the opportunities of His associates, His companions, His sons, His daughters. These are ever spoken of as One.

Then there came that as sought for self-indulgence, self-glorification; and there was the beginning of warring among themselves for activity—*still* in Spirit.

Then those that had made selfish movements moved into that which was and is *opportunity*, and there came life into same.

Then what was the Spirit that moved that made rebellion? The Spirit of God or the Spirit of Self?

This becomes self-evident even when we look about us in our own experience day by day. They that have the Spirit of God have the Spirit of Truth, have the Spirit of Christ, have the Spirit of Construction.

They that have the Spirit of Rebellion have the Spirit of Hate, the Spirit of Confusion; and seek self-glory rather than peace, harmony and understanding.

Thus as has been indicated, the Spirit pushed into matter—and became what we see in our three-dimensional world as the kingdoms of the earth; the mineral, the vegetable, the animal—a three-dimensional world.

And that which beareth witness is the Spirit of Truth, the Spirit of Light. For He said, "Let there be light; and there was light."

Then indeed there is no power that emanates that is not from God.

Then what is this Spirit of Rebellion, what is this Spirit of Hate? What is this Spirit of Self-Indulgence? What is this Spirit that makes men afraid?

Selfishness! Allowed, yes, of the Father. For, as given, He has not willed that the souls should perish but that we each should know the truth—and the truth would make us free. Of what? Selfishness!

Then we should each know that the sin which lies at our door is ever the sin of selfishness, self-glory, self-honor.

Hence as the Master has said, unless we become even as He, we may not in *any* wise enter in.

Enter to what? To the consciousness that our Father would that we be even as that Spirit of Truth manifested by the Son of Righteousness, that—even as those souls took on flesh in this three-dimensional world; becoming a part, a parcel of what? Those kingdoms of which the earth is a part; or that by their very presence is in existence.

Hence we find He had come, is come, ever has come into the experience that He might through love—not force, not hate, not by command but by edification and justification—bring that soul that is dominated by the Spirit to understanding.

Thus we find His intervention in man's attempt throughout the eons of time and space. For these (time and space) become portions of this three-dimensional plane. And what is the other? Time, Space, Patience!

For God has shown and does show us day by day, even as His Son gave, that in patience we become aware of our souls, of our identity, of our being each a corpuscle, as it were, in the great body, in the heart of, our God. And He has not willed otherwise.

Then what is the Spirit of God? *Patience, time and space* in the material understanding.

This then is our first premise; that God *is*—in the material experience of man—*time, space, patience!*

For have not even our own wise ones conceived that those elements between that which is and that which will be are of the same? What? God, the Spirit!

We in our seeking then have seen the movements in the earth, by the very activities of those influences, by what? "Where two or three are gathered together in my name, there am I in the midst of them." Either to do good or to do evil, according to our individual application of the Spirit of Truth or of Creative Force in our material experience.

Who then is the aggressor? He that seeks to glorify self, to make the selfish motives guide the progress.

And as has so oft been given in times past, God has winked at and God has allowed such things to pass; yet ever is calling—calling—to the sons of God; that we make straight the paths! For He will not *always* hold to those things that rend the heart of God.

For when we are raised in power we know, as we have seen, that our spirit beareth witness with *His spirit* that we are His children.

What then is the Spirit of Patriotism, the Spirit of Christ—yes, the Spirit of Knowledge, but that—as they are individualized by the activity of those that seek to know and make the paths straight—they take on that power, that might, yes that glory, that is the magnifying of that Spirit of Truth that is God in any individual group, nation or experience of man?

These then become those basic beginnings.

Now we, in our individual selves, seek—for what? Self-glory, self-understanding; or that we may be in His place as an emissary, a missionary, a *channel* through which *others*, too, may know that the consciousness of Christ is but that we have effaced self and are again one with Him—to be a purpose in the scheme of redemption for those souls whose spirits are a portion of the God as ourselves?

Let us indeed know then that God is not mocked, and that what we sow we must meet in our own selves. For He calls always unto all men to Come—*Come*—and take of the water of life.

What is this water of life? What is this that the Spirit and the Bride, or the Spirit and the Lamb, say to come and take of freely?

Patience, time, space! That we may know ourselves to be His; that our spirits, our souls, bear witness in the things that we do in which we bear witness of Him.

For that which has a beginning must have an ending. Hence rebellion and hate and selfishness must be wiped away, and *with it* will go sorrow and tears and sadness. For *only* good shall rule. For it is the Spirit of God that will move over the face of the earth, and Lo, His Son—even Jesus, the Christ—has borne in himself all these things, and has committed unto us the keeping of His sheep, His lambs, till He come to make an accounting with each of us.

Where—Where—Where will we be?

Reading 5755–1

GC: In all Life Readings given through this channel there are references to sojourns of the soul-entity between incarnations on the earth plane, in various planes of consciousness represented by the other planets in our solar system. You will give at this time a discourse which will explain what takes place in soul development in each of these states of consciousness in their order relative to the evolution of the soul; explaining what laws govern this movement from plane to plane, their influence on life in this earth plane and what if any relationship these planes have to astrology. Questions.

EC: Yes, we have the information and sources from which same may be obtained as to individual experiences, sojourns and their influence.

As we find, in attempting to give a coherent explanation of that as may be sought, or as may be made applicable in the experience of individuals who seek to apply such information, it is well that an individual soul-entity, the record of whose astrological and earthly sojourns you have, be used as an example.

Then a comparison may be drawn for those who would judge same from the astrological aspects, as well as from the astrological or planetary sojourns of such individuals.

What better example may be used, then, than this entity with whom you are dealing [EC]? [Case [294]]

Rather than the aspects of the material sojourn, then, we would give them from the astrological:

From an astrological aspect, then, the greater influence at the entrance of this entity that ye call Cayce was from Uranus. Here we find the extremes. The sojourn in Uranus was arrived at from what type of experience or activity of the entity? As Bainbridge, the entity in the material sojourn was a wastrel, one who considered only self; having to know the extremes in the own experience as well as others. Hence the entity was drawn to that environ. Or, how did the Master put it? "As the tree falls, so does it lie." [Eccl. 11:3 by Solomon. Where did Jesus say it?] Then in the Uranian sojourn there are the influences from the astrological aspects of *extremes*; and counted in thy own days from the very position of that attunement, that tone, that color. For it is not strange that music, color, vibration are all a part of the planets, just as the planets are a part—and a pattern—of the whole universe. Hence to that attunement which it had merited, which it had meted in itself, was the entity drawn for the experience. What form, what shape?

The birth of the entity into Uranus was not from the earth into Uranus, but from those stages of consciousness through which each entity or soul passes. It passes into oblivion as it were, save for its consciousness that there is a way, there is a light, there is an understanding, there have been failures and there are needs for help. Then help *consciously* is sought!

Hence the entity passes along those stages that some have seen as planes, some have seen as steps, some have seen as cycles, and some have experienced as places.

How far? How far is tomorrow to any soul? How far is yesterday from thy consciousness?

You are *in* same (that is, all time as one time), yet become gradually aware of it; passing through, then, as it were, God's record or book of consciousness or of remembrance; for meeting, being measured out as it were to that to which thou hast attained.

Who hath sought? Who hath understood?

Only they that seek shall find!

Then, born in what body? That as befits that plane of consciousness; the *extremes*, as ye would term same.

As to what body—what has thou abused? What hast thou used? What hast thou applied? What has thou neglected in thy extremes, thy extremities?

These are consciousnesses, these are bodies.

To give them form or shape—you have no word, you have no form in a three-dimensional world or plane of consciousness to give it to one in the seventh—have you?

Hence that's the form—we might say—"Have You?"

What is the form of this in thy consciousness? It rather indicates that everyone is questioned, "Have you?—Have You?"

That might be called the form. It is that which is thy concept of that being asked thyself—not that ye have formed of another.

With that sojourn then the entity finds need for, as it were, the giving expression of same again (the answering of "Have You?") in that sphere of consciousness in which there is a way in and through which one may become aware of the experience, the expression and the manifesting of same in a three-dimensional plane.

Hence the entity was born into the earth under what signs? Pisces, ye say. Yet astrologically from the records, these are some two signs off in thy reckoning.

Then from what is the influence drawn? Not merely because Pisces is accredited with an influence of such a nature, but because it *is*! And the "Have You" becomes then "There Is" or "I Am" in materiality or flesh, or material forces—even as He who has passed this way!

The entity as Bainbridge was born in the English land under the *sign*, as ye would term, of Scorpio; or from Venus as the second influence.

We find that the activity of the same entity in the earthly experience before that, in a French sojourn, followed the entrance into Venus.

What was the life there? How the application?

A child of love! A child of love—the most hopeful of all experiences of any that may come into a material existence; and to some in the earth that most dreaded, that most feared!

(These side remarks become more overburdening than what you are trying to obtain! but you've opened a big subject, haven't you?)

In Venus the body-form is near to that in the three dimensional plane. For it is what may be said to be rather *all*-inclusive! For it is that ye would call love—which, to be sure, may be licentious, selfish; which also may be so large, so inclusive as to take on the less of self and more of the ideal, more of that which is *giving*.

What is love? Then what is Venus? It is beauty, love, hope, charity—yet all of these have their extremes. But these extremes are not in the expressive nature or manner as may be found in that tone or attunement of Uranus; for they (in Venus) are more in the order that they blend as one with another.

So the entity passed through that experience, and on entering into materiality abused same; as the wastrel who sought those expressions of same in the loveliness for self alone, without giving—giving of self in return for same.

Hence we find the influences wielded in the sojourn of the entity from the astrological aspects or emotions of the mental nature are the ruling, yet must be governed by a standard.

And when self is the standard, it becomes very distorted in materiality.

Before that we find the influence was drawn for a universality of activity from Jupiter; in those experiences of the entity's sojourn or activity as the minister or teacher in Lucius. For the entity gave for the gospel's sake, a love, an activity and a hope through things that had become as of a universal nature.

Yet coming into the Roman influence from the earthly sojourn in Troy, we find that the entity through the Jupiterian environment was trained—as we understand—by being tempered to give self from the very universality, the very bigness of those activities in Jupiter.

For the sojourn in Troy was as the soldier, the carrying out of the order given, with a claim for activities pertaining to world affairs—a spreading.

What form, ye ask, did he take? That which may be described as in the circle with the dot, in which there is the turning within ever if ye will know the answer to thy problems; no matter in what stage of thy consciousness ye may be. For "Lo, I meet thee *within* thy holy temple," is the promise.

And the pattern is ever, "have you?" In other words, have you love? or the circle within, and not for self? but that He that giveth power, that meeteth within, may be magnified? Have you rather abased self that the glory may be magnified that thou didst have with Him before the worlds were, before a division of consciousness came?

Reading 3976-29

When there came about the periods of man's evolution in the earth, what was given then as to why man must be separated into tongues, into nations, into groups? "Lest they in their foolish wisdom defy God." What is here then intimated? That man, seeking his own gratification of the lusts of the flesh, might even in the earth defy God. With what, then, has man been endowed by his Creator? All that would be necessary for each individual soul-entity to be a companion with God. And that is God's desire toward man.

Thus when man began to defy God in the earth and the confusion arose which is represented in the Tower of Babel—these are representations of what was then the basis, the beginnings of nations. Nations were set up then in various portions of the land, and each group, one stronger than another, set about to seek their gratifications. Very few—yea, as ye will recall, it even became necessary that from one of these groups one individual, a man, be called. His ways were changed. His name was changed. Did it take sin away from the man, or was it only using that within the individual heart and purpose and desire even then, as man throughout the periods of unfoldment put—in his interpretation—that of material success first? It isn't that God chose to reserve or save anything that was good from man, so long as man was, is, and will be one who uses that living soul as a companion with God. That's God's purpose. That should be man's purpose.

In the application of this principle, then, in the present day what has come about? Each nation has set some standard of some activity of man as its idea, either of man's keeping himself for himself or of those in such other nations as man's preparation for that companionship with God. For remember, there are unchangeable laws. For God is law. Law is God. Love is law. Love is God. There are then in the hearts, the minds of man, various concepts of these laws and as to where and to what they are applicable. Then, just as in the days of old, the nature of the flesh, human flesh and its natures, has not changed, but the spirit maketh alive. The truth maketh one free. Just as man has done throughout the ages, so in the present, as one takes those of the various nations as have seen the light and have, through one form or another, sought to establish as the idea of that nation, of that people, some symbol that has and does represent those peoples in those days of the fathers of the present land called America.

What is the spirit of America? Most individuals proudly boast "freedom." Freedom of what? When ye bind men's hearts and minds through various ways and manners, does it give them freedom of speech? Freedom of worship? Freedom from want? Not unless those basic principles are applicable throughout the tenets and lines as has been set, but with that principle freedom. For God meant man to be free and thus gave man will, a will even to defy God. *God* has not willed that any soul should perish, but hath with every trial or temptation prepared a way of escape.

There have come through the various periods of man's unfoldment, teachers proclaiming "This the way, here the manner in which ye may know," and yet in the Teacher of Teachers is found the way, He who even in Himself fulfilled the law. For when God said, "Let there be light" there came Light into that which He had created, that was without form and was void and it became the Word, and the Word dwelt among men and men perceived it not. The Word today dwells among men and many men perceive it not.

Those nations who have taken those vows that man shall be free should also take those vows "He shall know the truth and the truth then shall make him free."

Then what is this that would be given thee today? Here is thy lesson: Hear ye all! Beware lest ye as an individual soul, a son, a daughter of God, fail in thy mission in the earth today; that those ye know, those ye contact shall know the truth of God, not by thy word, bombastic words, but in longsuffering, in patience, in harmony, that ye create in thine own lives, for it must begin with thee. God has shown thee the pattern, even one Jesus, who became the Christ that ye might have an advocate with the Father, for the Father hath said "In the day ye eat or use the knowledge for thine own aggrandizement, ye shall die." But he that had persuaded the spirit, the souls that God had brought into being, to push into matter to gratify desire for self-expression, self-indulgence, self-satisfaction, said "Ye shall not surely die", or what were then the activities of man—for as had been said, "A day is a thousand years, a thousand years as a day."

What was the length of life then? Nearly a thousand years. What is your life today? May it not be just as He had given, just as He indicated to those peoples, just as He did to the lawgiver, just as He did to David—first from a thousand years to a hundred and twenty, then to eighty? Why? Why? The sin of man in his desire for self-gratification.

What nations of the earth today vibrate to those things that they have and are creating in their own land, their own environment? Look to the nations where the span of life has been extended from sixty to eight-four years. You will judge who is serving God. These are judgements. These are the signs to those who seek to know, who will study the heavens, who will analyze the elements, who will know the heart of man, they that seek to know the will of the Father for themselves answer "Lord, here am I, use me, send me where I am needed . . . "

Then apply in thine own life truth. What is truth? It might have been answered, had an individual entity who stood at the crossways of the world waited for an answer. Yet that soul had purified itself and had given the new commandment that "ye love one another!"

What is it all about then? "Thou shalt love the Lord thy God with all thine heart, thine soul, thine mind, thine body, and thy neighbor as thyself." The rest of all the theories that may be concocted by man are nothing, if these are just lived. Love thy neighbor as thyself in the associations day by day, preferring as did the Christ who died on the cross rather than preferring the world be His without a struggle.

Know, then, that as He had His cross, so have you. May you take it with a smile. You can, if ye will let Him bear it with thee. Do it.

Reading 262–88

GC: You will have before you the Norfolk Study Group #1, members of which are present here and their work on the lesson Destiny. You will give any suggestions that will be helpful in completing the section on Destiny of the Body, and continue with a discourse on the Destiny of the Soul. You will answer the questions that may be asked.

EC: Yes, we have the group as gathered here and the work on the lesson Destiny, as a group and as individuals.

That which has been gathered from the information, from the experiences, as compiled, is very good—as we find. There needs be only, then, a correlating or tying together—as it were—of that which has been compiled or gathered together; as of the Mind and of the Body, for these are as one. For Mind ever is the builder; hence man in the

mental sphere, man in the material sphere, must make for that experience where the Body and the Mind are as one and not warring one
with another; so that the consciousness of the Spirit of Truth is ever the
motivative influence in the experience of the individual in its activities.
How was He in the hour of trial, of temptation? He gave the lesson as
to how that even though the body would be destroyed, in three days
it would be raised again. He gave the lesson as to how there should
be the thought of the fellow man, when those upon whom He had
depended to be the ministers in His stead failed to catch the vision of
what it was all about. He healed even His enemies, thus making the
Mind and the Body as one; even in those hours when the change and
the dissolution, the enlightening, the resurrection, were taking place
within the activities of the *mental* body, expressing themselves through
the activities of the material body.

So ye in making for that which may be helpful to thy fellow man in
the application of the lesson, let all be of one Mind—even as in Christ,
who thought it not robbery to be equal with God, yet desiring ever
that *His* followers, *His* brethren, *His* friends, be one with Him, equal to
and one with the Father.

So may ye, in the manners as indicated that the activities of the Body
bear within themselves the fruits of the Spirit, attune the material forces
in such ways and manners that the *mind* changeth ever to become in
accord with, in attune with, whatever, wherever, in whatever manner it
is presented with those influences that reach *in*, that are from without,
that must be coordinated; that the Body, the Mind, may be carried to
the Creative Forces—in what?

The Destiny, then, of the Soul. Each individual as a child of the Creative Force came into being that it, that child, might be a companion
with the Creative Force, God, in its activity; given by the very breath, by
the desire, by the will of the Father that with which it might be one with
the Father. Not the Body as manifested in the flesh; not the Mind alone
that may partake of all those environs through which it passes; but the
Soul, which is as lasting as eternity, as the Creative Force, as the Creative
Energy, as God Himself; that we through Him might know ourselves
to be one with Him. He hath not willed that any Soul should perish.

Then, the Destiny of the Soul—as of all creation—is to be one with
Him; continually growing, growing, for that association. What seeth

man in nature? What seeth man in those influences that he becomes aware of? Change, ever; change, ever. Man hath termed this evolution, growth, life itself; but it continues to enter. That force, that power which manifests itself in separating—or as separate forces and influences in the earth, continues to enter; and then change; continuing to pour in and out. From whence came it? Whither does it go when it returns?

So the Soul's activity in the earth, as it is seen in this or that phase of experience, is that it may be one with the Creative Forces, the Creative Energies.

Many questions, then, are brought to thine own consciousness that must be answered *within* thine inner self; having to do with thine own experiences.

Then, seek ye within thine own consciousness. There may then be given that as may be helpful in thine interpretation of thine experiences; that may bring a consciousness to thy fellow man of the awareness of His presence and of the Soul's returning to that oneness with Him.

Reading 900-348

This then the final end of each individual soul or being in its evolution to that from which it (the soul) radiated in the beginning, for through the various phases as have been given we find each building, little by little, line upon line, precept upon precept, becoming one *with* the whole, yet not the whole within itself, but within itself wholly within the whole.

EDGAR CAYCE'S A.R.E.

Who Was Edgar Cayce?
Twentieth Century Psychic and Medical Clairvoyant

Edgar Cayce (pronounced Kay-Cee, 1877-1945) has been called the "sleeping prophet," the "father of holistic medicine," and the most-documented psychic of the 20th century. For more than 40 years of his adult life, Cayce gave psychic "readings" to thousands of seekers while in an unconscious state, diagnosing illnesses and revealing lives lived in the past and prophecies yet to come. But who, exactly, was Edgar Cayce?

Cayce was born on a farm in Hopkinsville, Kentucky, in 1877, and his psychic abilities began to appear as early as his childhood. He was able to see and talk to his late grandfather's spirit, and often played with "imaginary friends" whom he said were spirits on the other side. He also displayed an uncanny ability to memorize the pages of a book simply by sleeping on it. These gifts labeled the young Cayce as strange, but all Cayce really wanted was to help others, especially children.

Later in life, Cayce would find that he had the ability to put himself into a sleep-like state by lying down on a couch, closing his eyes, and folding his hands over his stomach. In this state of relaxation and meditation, he was able to place his mind in contact with all time and space—the universal consciousness, also known as the super-conscious mind. From there, he could respond to questions as broad as, "What are the secrets of the universe?" and "What is my purpose in life?" to as specific as, "What can I do to help my arthritis?" and "How were the pyramids of Egypt built?" His responses to these questions came to be called "readings," and their insights offer practical help and advice to individuals even today.

The majority of Edgar Cayce's readings deal with holistic health and the treatment of illness. Yet, although best known for this material, the sleeping Cayce did not seem to be limited to concerns about the physical body. In fact, in their entirety, the readings discuss an astonishing 10,000 different topics. This vast array of subject matter can be narrowed down into a smaller group of topics that, when compiled together, deal with the following five categories: (1) Health-Related Information; (2) Philosophy and Reincarnation; (3) Dreams and Dream Interpretation; (4) ESP and Psychic Phenomena; and (5) Spiritual Growth, Meditation, and Prayer.

Learn more at EdgarCayce.org.

What Is A.R.E.?

Edgar Cayce founded the non-profit Association for Research and Enlightenment (A.R.E.) in 1931, to explore spirituality, holistic health, intuition, dream interpretation, psychic development, reincarnation, and ancient mysteries—all subjects that frequently came up in the more than 14,000 documented psychic readings given by Cayce.

The Mission of the A.R.E. is to help people transform their lives for the better, through research, education, and application of core concepts found in the Edgar Cayce readings and kindred materials that seek to manifest the love of God and all people and promote the purposefulness of life, the oneness of God, the spiritual nature of humankind, and the connection of body, mind, and spirit.

With an international headquarters in Virginia Beach, Va., a regional headquarters in Houston, regional representatives throughout the U.S., Edgar Cayce Centers in more than thirty countries, and individual members in more than seventy countries, the A.R.E. community is a global network of individuals.

A.R.E. conferences, international tours, camps for children and adults, regional activities, and study groups allow like-minded people to gather for educational and fellowship opportunities worldwide.

A.R.E. offers membership benefits and services that include a quarterly body-mind-spirit member magazine, Venture Inward, a member newsletter covering the major topics of the readings, and access to the entire set of readings in an exclusive online database.

Learn more at EdgarCayce.org.

EDGARCAYCE.ORG